DANGER ZONE

\MAZING SPIDER-MAN #692-694

Vriter: **DAN SLOTT**
enciler: **HUMBERTO RAMOS**
ıker: **VICTOR OLAZABA**
olorist: **EDGAR DELGADO**
etterer: **VC'S CHRIS ELIOPOULOS**

\VENGING SPIDER-MAN #11

Vriter: **ZEB WELLS**
rtist: **STEVE DILLON**
olorist: **FRANK MARTIN JR.**
etterer: **VC'S CHRIS ELIOPOULOS**

MAZING SPIDER-MAN #695-697

riter: **DAN SLOTT** & **CHRISTOS GAGE**
nciler: **GIUSEPPE CAMUNCOLI**
er: **DAN GREEN**
olorist: **ANTONIO FABELA**
tterer: **VC'S CHRIS ELIOPOULOS**

sistant Editor: **ELLIE PYLE** • Associate Editor: **SANA AMANAT**
itor: **STEPHEN WACKER** • Executive Editor: **TOM BREVOORT**

dicated to Steve, Stan, John, Gil, Roy, Gerry, Ross and everyone who paved the way.

lection Editor: **JENNIFER GRÜNWALD** • Assistant Editors: **ALEX STARBUCK** & **NELSON RIBEIRO**
tor, Special Projects: **MARK D. BEAZLEY** • Senior Editor, Special Projects: **JEFF YOUNGQUIST**
iior Vice President of Sales: **DAVID GABRIEL** • SVP of Brand Planning & Communications: **MICHAEL PASCIULLO**

or in Chief: **AXEL ALONSO** • Chief Creative Officer: **JOE QUESADA** • Publisher: **DAN BUCKLEY** • Executive Producer: **ALAN FINE**

R-MAN: DANGER ZONE. Contains material originally published in magazine form as AMAZING SPIDER-MAN #692-697 and AVENGING SPIDER-MAN #11. First printing 2012. Hardcover ISBN# 978-0-7851-6009-0. er ISBN# 978-0-7851-6010-6. Published by MARVEL WORLDWIDE, INC., a subsidiary of MARVEL ENTERTAINMENT, LLC. OFFICE OF PUBLICATION: 135 West 50th Street, New York, NY 10020. Hardcover: $24.99 per copy in the U.S. and $27.99 in Canada (GST #R127032852). Softcover: $19.99 per copy in the U.S. and $21.99 in Canada (GST #R127032852). n Agreement #40668537. **Printed in the U.S.A.** ALAN P - Office of the President, Marvel Worldwide, Inc. and EVP & CMO Marvel Characters B.V.; DAN BUCKLEY, Publisher & President - Print, Animation & Digital Divisions; JOE QUESADA, Chief Creative Officer; TOM RT, SVP of Publishing; DAVID BOGART, SVP of Operations & Procurement, Publishing; RUWAN JAYATILLEKE, SVP & Associate Publisher, Publishing; C.B. CEBULSKI, SVP of Creator & Content Development; DAVID ., SVP of Publishing Sales & Circulation; MICHAEL PASCIULLO, SVP of Brand Planning & Communications; JIM O'KEEFE, VP of Operations & Logistics; DAN CARR, Executive Director of Publishing Technology; SUSAN Editorial Operations Manager; ALEX MORALES, Publishing Operations Manager; STAN LEE, Chairman Emeritus. For information regarding advertising in Marvel Comics or on Marvel.com, please contact Niza Disla, of Marvel Partnerships, at ndisla@marvel.com. For Marvel subscription inquiries, please call 800-217-9158. **Manufactured between 10/15/2012 and 11/26/2012 (hardcover), and 10/15/2012 and 5/20/2013 ver), by R.R. DONNELLEY, INC., SALEM, VA, USA.**

654321

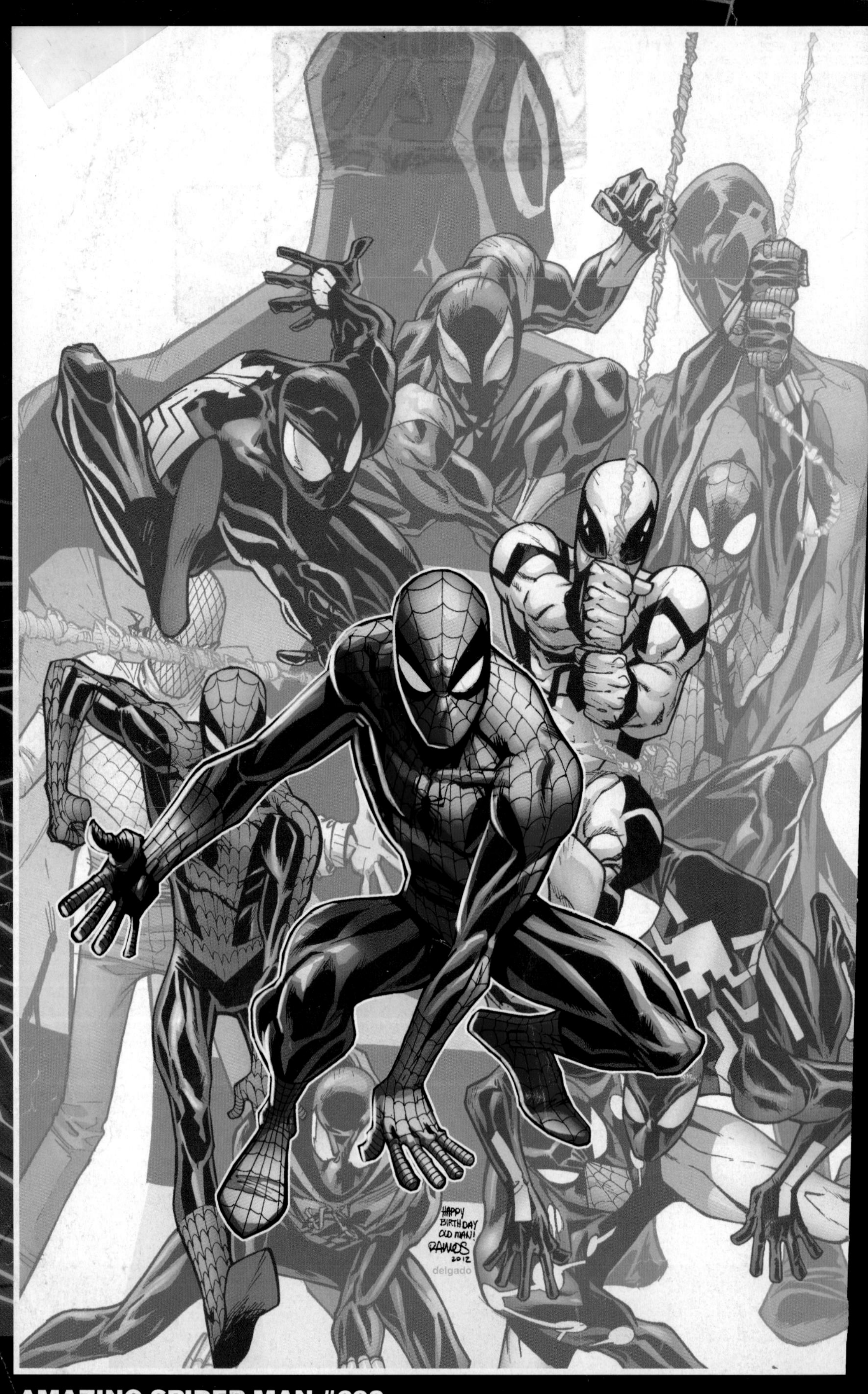

AMAZING SPIDER-MAN #692
COVER BY HUMBERTO RAMOS & EDGAR DELGADO

Today.
NO FOOD IN THE FRIDGE
JUST GREAT.
AND LEMME GUESS...
YEP. NO ONE SIGNED MY FORM.
RRRRAY MAGUIRE. THERE.
BOLD MOVE, SIR. GOING OUTSIDE THE LINES.
OH, LIKE ANYONE'S GONNA CHECK...
"...OR PAY THE SLIGHTEST ATTENTION TO ME. STILL...
"...FEELS PRETTY GOOD. I SHOULD JUST GO WITH IT. DO SOMETHING FOR ONCE IN MY LIFE."
UM...HEY, CHRISSY...
SCHOOL
...I WAS JUST--
TUMP
...FADES BACK AND MAKES THE CATCH!
IT WAS SWEET!
HEY, IT WAS ALL YOU.
HUNSACKER.
NICE.
GUESS YOU DIDN'T SEE ME THERE. UM. LITTLE HELP?
HERE.
THANKS.
NO PROB. C'MON. YOU DO NOT WANNA MISS THIS!
NOW THIS? THIS IS PETER PARKER, THE ONE-AND-ONL AMAZING SPIDER-MAN. AND TODAY SHOULD BE--
TODAY'S GONNA BE THE BEST DAY OF MY LIFE!

KNOW ABOUT ANDY:
HIS MOM, ALICE? NOT THE MOST HANDS-ON PARENT.
ANDY?! YOU UP YET? GET DOWN HERE AND EAT SOMETHING.
WE'RE LEAVING IN TEN. WITH OR WITHOUT YOU.
WHU?
HIS DAD, RAY? NOT MUCH BETTER.
#1 MOM
--STAYING LATE WITH THE NEW CLIENTS.
AGAIN?
YOU WANTED TO REMODEL THE UPSTAIRS. NOT ME.
GUYS? ANYONE SIGN THAT PERMISSION SLIP?
I NEED IT FOR THE CLASS TRIP TOMORROW. HELLO?
AND THE FACULTY AT MIDTOWN HIGH... DOESN'T REALLY KNOW WHAT TO DO WITH HIM EITHER.
STRAIGHT C STUDENT. LOUSY SATS. NO EXTRACURRICULARS.
MAGUIRE, HOW DO YOU EXPECT TO GET INTO COLLEGE WITH THIS?
I DUNNO.
ANDY MAGUIRE ISN'T REALLY THE KIND OF KID WHO STANDS OUT THAT MUCH.
WHOA. CHRISSY CHEN IS SO DAMN CUTE...
...IN A NERDY/ASIAN/TINA FEY KINDA WAY.
AND SHE'S TOTALLY INTO SUPER HEROES. LIKE ME! C'MON, I CAN DO THIS.
AND THERE'S A REASON FOR THAT.
STANDING OUT MEANS TAKING A RISK. LEAVING YOURSELF OPEN TO FAIL.
AN, LOOK AT MARK NSACKER. HE'S THE EW KID. HASN'T EVEN BEEN HERE TWO WEEKS...
...AND HE'S DATING PAULA LAKE. HEAD CHEERLEADER. HOTTEST GIRL IN SCHOOL.
HOW DOES HE DO THAT?
GOD, HOW I HATE 'IM.
YOU SEE, FOR ANDY, THOUGH HE'D NEVER ADMIT IT, NOT FAILING IS GOOD ENOUGH.
AND THAT'S WHY HE'S NO PETER PARKER.
WHY HE'S NOT A NERD.
JOCK.
BAND GEEK.
POSER.
STONER.
OR MUCH OF ANYTHING, GOOD OR BAD. HE'S JUST... THERE.
BUT ALL THAT'S ABOUT TO CHANGE...

BOTH OF YOU, STOP THIS! THEY'VE TAKEN THE KEY!
I DON'T CARE WHAT GRUDGES YOU HOLD FOR EACH OTHER. GET THEM...OR MAKE AN ENEMY OF ME!
WHAT?
NO. THAT'S MINE TOO.
LISTEN, PUNK. YOU EVER WANT TO SEE THAT GIRL AGAIN, YOU'LL HELP ME GET THE KEY BACK.
HOW ABOUT THIS? WE BOTH WANT THE KEY...

OCKED. AYBE I CAN--
LET ME. I HAVE JUST THE THING.
SPIDER-ISLAND... YES. IF I HADN'T SEEN YOU AND SPIDER-MAN TOGETHER THEN, I'D ALMOST--
HAAAII--!
--MMFF!
THWIP
THWIP
ALMOST WHAT?
NOTHING.
LET'S GO!

EH--?

THE KEY! GET THEM!
HOLD THIS, MAX. I'M GONNA NEED BOTH HANDS FREE...

...TO DO THIS!
OH!

YOU'RE GOOD WITH THOSE.
I GOT A LOT OF PRACTICE DURING THAT SPIDER-ISLAND THING.

YES! AILED IT!
NO! YOU IDIOTS! THAT'S THE CENTRAL TRANSMITTER!
TIBERIUS STONE? W-WHAT--
C'MON, MAX. THIS IS OUR CHANCE TO BAIL.
ARE YOU SURE YOU'RE UP TO IT?
NEVER FELT BETTER. IN FACT...
...MY PRACTICE SESSIONS ARE COMING BACK TO ME.
THWIP
BRAKOOSH
YOINK!

MAX, IN CASE SOMETHING HAPPENS TO ME...THIS IS HOW YOU ADJUST THE WEB-SHOOTERS.
I'M SETTING THIS ONE FOR AN *ULTRA-THIN STRAND.*
PETER, YOUR NOSE IS *BLEEDING!*
MAX, PLEASE... I'VE GOT TO CONCENTRATE.
I'LL ONLY GET ONE SHOT AT THIS...
THWIP
WHAT--?
TNNG

SSASH
OOK AT YOU. 'OU'RE LIKE A SSETTE TAPE. NDA FUN IN A NOSTALGIC WAY...
...BUT USELESS!
JUST 'CAUSE YOU CAN'T APPRECIATE SOMETHING DOESN'T MAKE IT USELESS. IT MAKES YOU STUPID AND IMPATIENT, LIKE YOUR WHOLE GENERATION...
...PHIL.
YOU KNOW?
I KNOW MORE THAN THAT, PUNK. I'VE GOT A LOCK ON YOUR LITTLE PIECE OF FLUFF, NORAH WINTERS...
...AND IF I SAY THE WORD, SHE DIES.
SHE'S MINE, YOU HAS-BEEN! YOU LAY A HAND ON HER AND I'LL--

PETER, THIS IS OUR CHANCE!
HOLD ON, I'LL UNTIE YOU--
WAY AHEAD OF YOU. THERE WAS, UH, A NAIL. I WAS WAITING FOR AN OPENING.
BUT THIS ISN'T IT. THERE'S A DOZEN NINJAS BETWEEN US AND THE DOOR.
WHAT WERE YOU THINKING? WHY DIDN'T YOU CALL THE COPS, THE AVENGERS--
THEY SAID IF I DID THEY'D KNOW, AND THEY'D KILL YOU.
AND YOU FELL FOR IT? YOU'RE SUPPOSED TO BE A GENIUS!
I DIDN'T BLINDLY FOLLOW THEIR ORDERS. I CAME ARMED.
YOU'RE KIDDING ME. MAX MODELL IS PACKING?
IN A MANNER OF SPEAKING. THESE ARE SPIDER-MAN'S WEB-SHOOTERS, AREN'T THEY?
GOOD IDEA. I'VE HAD SOME PRACTICE...DURING THE TESTING PHASE.
BUT MY HEAD'S SPLITTING... AND NO WONDER, THERE'S REAL DANGER ALL AROUND.

...SO YOU'RE A DEAD MAN!
WAIT.
THIS SHOULD BE... AMUSING.

OR MAYBE THAT KEY'S A KNOCKOFF. I DOUBT YOU COULD TELL.
I MEAN, YOU OBVIOUSLY DON'T KNOW THE REAL HOBGOBLIN FROM A CHEAP IMITATION.
YOU GOTTA BE KIDDING.
IF THERE'S A KNOCKOFF HERE, IT'S YOU, PAL.
'CAUSE I KILLED THE OLD HOBGOBLIN...BUT I DON'T MIND DOING IT AGAIN!
MY NAME'S RODERICK KINGSLEY. THAT WAS MY BROTHER YOU KILLED.
WHICH, HONESTLY, I'M FINE WITH. HE WAS AN IDIOT.
BUT THEN YOU WENT TOO FAR...
YOU STOLE MY BRAND...

ENOUGH OF THIS CHARADE. SPIDER-MAN WOULD ***NEVER*** ENDANGER AN OLD FOOL LIKE YOU WHEN HE COULD COME HIMSELF.

WAIT! I'M AN INVENTOR. IF YOU LET US GO, I'LL HELP YOU DISARM THE CASE. IT'S BOOBY-TRAPPED...IT'LL KILL WHOEVER OPENS IT-- I'M ***NOT*** LYING ABOUT THAT.

I KNOW.

FUJIWARA.

YOU HONOR ME, MASTER.

AAIEEEGGHH

VVZZRRAKK!

AT LAST...

MASTER, A MAN IS AT THE GATE. HE HAS BROUGHT THE CASE.
SPIDER-MAN?
DOUBTFUL.
"HE IS OLD, FAT AND WEAK."
N-NOW YOU LISTEN TO ME... I'VE GOT WHAT YOU ASKED FOR, BUT I'M NO FOOL. SPIDER-MAN IS WITH ME. HE'S WATCHING, TO MAKE SURE THERE AREN'T ANY TRICKS.
I'LL GIVE YOU THE CASE...AS SOON AS YOU PROVE TO ME PETER PARKER'S ALIVE.
PETER!
MAX? ARE YOU CRAZY? NOW THAT YOU'VE BROUGHT THEM WHAT THEY WANT, THEY'LL KILL US BOTH!
THEY WOULDN'T DARE. THE SITUATION'S UNDER CONTROL. SPIDER-MAN IS WATCHING.
I LOVE YOU FOR TRYING, MAX...BUT EVEN IF I WASN'T SPIDER-MAN, I'D KNOW YOU WERE BLUFFING. YOU LOOK LIKE YOU'RE DROWNING IN YOUR OWN SWEAT.
COULD'VE BROKEN FREE ANY TIME, BUT THE CONDITION I'M IN--WITH KINGPIN, HOBGOBLIN AND A BILLION NINJAS AROUND--I DON'T STAND A CHANCE.
BUT WITH MAX'S NECK ON THE CHOPPING BLOCK, I DON'T HAVE A CHOICE. JUST WISH I COULD THINK OF SOMETHING THAT WON'T GET US BOTH KILLED...

Columbia University Medical Center.
COMA WARD.
NOT A SHRED OF I.D. NOTHING BUT THE CELL PHONE SHE USED TO CALL 911.
WHICH WAS A BURNER...UNTRACEABLE. I COULD RUN HER FINGERPRINTS THROUGH A.F.I.S., SEE IF ANYTHING POPS.
I DON'T THINK THAT'LL WORK, CHUCK.

HE SKIN OVER HER GERTIPS HAS BEEN ANDED OFF. NOT LONG AGO.
THIS LADY REALLY DIDN'T WANT TO BE FOUND. QUESTION IS, WAS SHE RUNNING FROM US, OR SOMEONE ELSE? I'LL CHECK WANTED FUGITIVES.
DON'T FORGET HOSPITALS. SHE COULD BE RUNNING FROM HERSELF, IN A SENSE.

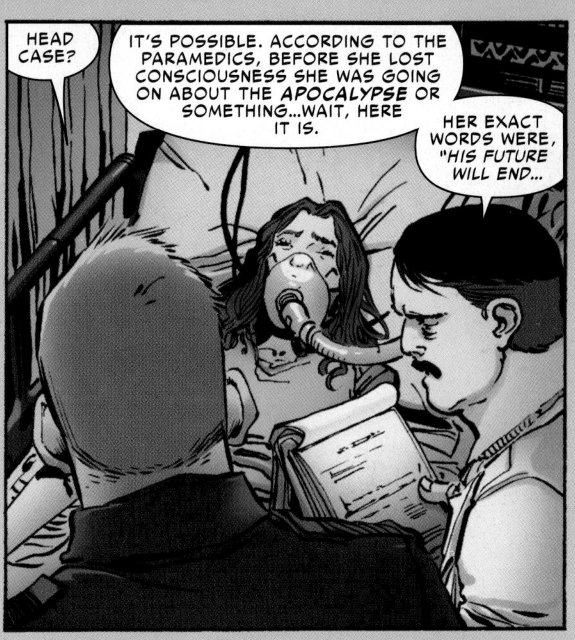
HEAD CASE?
IT'S POSSIBLE. ACCORDING TO THE PARAMEDICS, BEFORE SHE LOST CONSCIOUSNESS SHE WAS GOING ON ABOUT THE APOCALYPSE OR SOMETHING...WAIT, HERE IT IS.
HER EXACT WORDS WERE, "HIS FUTURE WILL END...

'...IN A FLASH OF GOLD.'

"RODRIGUEZ SAID SHE LOOKED TERRIFIED...

"...BUT SHE NEVER SAID OF WHAT."

I'M SORRY, PETER. I KNOW I PROMISED THE BLACK BOX WAS YOUR SANCTUARY. YOU MUST REALIZE I'D NEVER INVADE YOUR PRIVACY IF THERE WAS ANOTHER OPTION.
BUT IT'S WHERE YOU DO YOUR SPIDER-MAN WORK. IF THERE'S A WAY TO REACH HIM, IT'S GOT TO BE INSIDE. AND YOUR LIFE DEPENDS ON IT.
I'D LIKE TO THINK YOU'D BE IMPRESSED BY THE "ALL ACCESS" KEY.
IT USES LOCALIZED TACHYONS TO LOOK INTO THE PAST, DISCOVER WHAT CODE PATTERN WAS ENTERED MOST OFTEN...
...AND REPLICATE IT.
CLICK
OH... MY.
I KNOW THAT, IN A SENSE, YOU PREPARE SPIDER-MAN FOR BATTLE. BUT UNTIL JUST NOW, I NEVER THOUGHT OF HORIZON AS...MANUFACTURING WEAPONS.
NO TIME FOR THAT NOW. ESPECIALLY WHEN I THINK I JUST GOT LUCKY.
THIS MUST BE THE "CASE" THE KIDNAPPERS WANT; THE SECURITY TECH IS LIKE NOTHING ELSE HERE.
ALL RIGHT. CLEARLY I'D BE A FOOL TO TRUST THESE PEOPLE. AND THEY PROBABLY ARE WATCHING ME.
BUT I'D BET THE PEOPLE THEY USUALLY BLACKMAIL AREN'T GENIUS INVENTORS...

izon Labs.

SOUTH STREET SEAPORT.

HORIZON

To: mmodell@horizonlabs.com
From: pparker@horizonlabs.com
Re: Urgent - Eyes Only

OH, NO... PETER!

MODELL. FIRST THINGS FIRST. WE'RE WATCHING YOU. YOU CALL THE POLICE, THE AVENGERS, ANYONE...PARKER DIES. YOU FORWARD THIS EMAIL, HE DIES.
YOU MENTION THIS TO ANYBODY... WELL. YOU'RE A SMART GUY. YOU GET THE GIST.
WE GOT AN INSIDE SOURCE SAYS THAT YOU AND PARKER HAVE BOTH BEEN BUILDING TECH FOR THE SPIDER.

SO YOU GET AHOLD OF OL' WEB-HEAD. TELL HIM TO BRING THE CASE TO SHADOWLAND. ALONE. HE'LL KNOW WHAT YOU MEAN.
BUT I HAVE NO IDEA HOW TO REACH--
AND DO IT FAST. OR YOU'RE GONNA NEED TO TAKE OUT A "HELP WANTED" AD.

nts Later...
I DON'T THINK PETE'S IN TODAY, MAX.
THAT'S OKAY, UATU. I JUST NEED... SOME NOTES I LEFT IN THERE.
WE'VE BEEN COLLABORATING ON A PROJECT. UM, NOTHING I CAN DISCUSS YET...
UH-HUH.

UPID MISTAKE
BER TWO: NO
MAN'S WORTH
ETTING THAT
NG UP ON. IT
UST MAKES
YOU WEAK.
ALTHOUGH I GUESS THIS PARTICULAR WEAKNESS IS PRACTICALLY A TRADITION.
WE GOBLINS JUST CAN'T RESIST THE BLONDES.
BUT YOU SHOULD BE THROWING HER OFF A BRIDGE, NOT FOLLOWING HER AROUND LIKE A LOVESICK SCHOOLBOY.
KIDDO, YOU'RE DOING IT WRONG...
...AND IT'S WAY PAST TIME THE ORIGINAL HOBGOBLIN TOOK YOU TO SCHOOL.

"...WHERE THE HELL IS THAT THING?"

I MEAN, KEEPING YOUR GEAR IN YOUR *APARTMENT?* THAT'S WORSE THAN A ROOKIE MISTAKE. IT'S JUST *DUMB.*
AND IN THIS LINE OF WORK, IF YOU'RE *STUPID,* YOU PAY THE PRICE.

OLD ON. I THINK I JUST FOUND SOMETHING YOU CARE ABOUT *MORE.*

SOMEONE'S BEEN USING THE BAT-DRONE TO BE A *PEEPING TOM.* AH, KID. YOU GET MORE PATHETIC BY THE MINUTE.
BUT THAT PRETTY MUCH SETTLES IT.

INTERESTING. YOU, BOY...HOW DO YOU CONTACT SPIDER-MAN? SPEAK AS IF YOUR LIFE DEPENDS ON IT.
TIME TO PLAY A HUNCH. I'M GUESSING IT'S NO COINCIDENCE MY HEAD WENT WONKY RIGHT BEFORE HOBGOBLIN ATTACKED...
IT'S A SIGNAL. BASED ON THE SPIDER-SENSE THAT WARNS HIM OF DANGER. BUT RIGHT BEFORE YOUR GUY GRABBED ME, HE CALLED. SAID YOU'D DONE SOMETHING TO HIM.
...RAMPED HIS SPIDER-SENSE INTO OVERDRIVE. IT'S GOING OFF CONSTANTLY, IN RESPONSE TO THE TINIEST THREAT. MY SIGNAL CAN'T GET THROUGH. YOU'LL HAVE TO TURN IT OFF.
HMM...NO. NO, I DON'T THINK I WILL.
THIS IS GOOD NEWS FOR YOU, STONE. YOUR DEVICE FUNCTIONS PROPERLY. WHICH MEANS YOUR LEGS MAY CONTINUE TO AS WELL.
Y-YES, SIR. AND IF I MAY I THINK I KNOW HOW TO GET A MESSAGE TO SPIDER-MAN REGARDLESS BUT WE'LL NEED TO RECORD IT.
TIBERIUS STONE! I KNEW I SAW HIM WHEN I FOUGHT HOBGOBLIN.*
THAT TRAITOR'S BEEN WORKING FOR THE KINGPIN...SELLING HIM HORIZON LABS' SECRETS! I'M GONNA--
--I'M GONNA SIT TIGHT. 'CAUSE WITH THAT JAMMER ON, I CAN BARELY STAND.
LAST ISH. - S
BUT THE SECOND THEY GIVE ME AN OPENING...
I CAN RECORD A HOSTAGE VIDEO ON MY DRONE CAMERA. IT SHOULD BE AROUND... IT'S PROGRAMMED TO STAY CLOSE.
HEY...

...SPIDER-
AN'S BEST
FRIEND!
HE'S A SCIENTIST AT HORIZON LABS. BUILDS ALL OF THE WALL-CRAWLER'S TECH. HE'S VALUABLE TO HIM.
ALL WE GOTTA DO IS GET WORD OUT TO THE SPIDER. HE'LL TRADE THE "PACKAGE" FOR PARKER... OR WE OFF THE NERD. EITHER WAY, WE SCORE A WIN.
"PACKAGE"? HOBGOBLIN'S TALKING ABOUT THE BRIEFCASE I TOOK FROM HIM. WHATEVER IT IS, THE KINGPIN WANTS IT BAD.
JUST ONE PROBLEM. WHATEVER HAPPENED TO JACK UP MY SPIDER-SENSE HAS GIVEN ME THE MOTHER OF ALL MIGRAINES. I CAN'T FUNCTION.
AND THE ONLY WAY TO KEEP THESE GUYS FROM KILLING ME...IS FOR SPIDER-MAN TO SHOW UP WITH MY RANSOM.
EVEN BY THE STANDARDS OF MY USUAL PARKER LUCK, I AM ROYALLY SCREWED.
ANGER ZONE
ART TWO: KEY TO THE KINGDOM
AN SLOTT & RISTOS GAGE
WRITERS
GIUSEPPE CAMUNCOLI
PENCILS
DAN GREEN
INKS
ANTONIO FABELA
COLORS
VC'S CHRIS ELIOPOULOS
LETTERER
McNIVEN & WEST
COVER
E PYLE
AVERICK
STEPHEN WACKER
GOOSE
AXEL ALONSO
ICEMAN
JOE QUESADA
JESTER
DAN BUCKLEY
PUBLISHER
ALAN FINE
EXEC. PRODUCER

ort Authority Bus
erminal.
OVER HERE! IT JUST HAPPENED...SHE COLLAPSED, STARTED SEIZING--
FUTURE... DYING. EVERYTHING... ENDS. FLASH OF GOLD...
F.D. N.Y.
I'M... SO SORRY... PETER...
Shadowland.
THE KINGPIN'S STRONGHOLD IN THE HEART OF NEW YORK CITY.
HOBGOBLIN!
I HOPE, FOR YOUR SAKE, YOU HAVE AN EXTREMELY COMPELLING EXPLANATION...
...AS TO WHY YOU HAVE BROUGHT THIS...PERSON... HERE.
I GOT THE BEST EXPLANATION IN THE WORLD, BOSS. THIS IS PETER BENJAMIN PARKER.
AND HE'S THE KEY TO EVERYTHING. 'CAUSE BELIEVE IT OR NOT, THIS LITTLE GEEK IS...
NNGH... WHERE...?
SPIDER-SENSE IS STILL IN OVERDRIVE. HEAD'S POUNDING SO BAD IT'S HARD TO SEE...BUT I CAN TELL THIS IS NOT GOOD.

MNV SWEST

I FINALLY GOT ONE OVER ON YOU, SPIDER-MAN!
HAHAHAHAHAHA!
NEXT:
SPIDEY REVEALED
OH, WE'RE JUST GETTING STAR

US, PARKER. YOU
CAN DO THIS.
I'VE HAD YOUR
AD ZAPPED BY
ERYONE FROM
YSTERIO TO
D.D.O.K.
SHUT IT OUT. IGNORE IT.
THAT'S IT. NOW JUST PUT ONE FOOT IN FRONT OF THE OTHER...
NO WAY I CAN RISK WEB-SWINGING RIGHT NOW. I'LL TRY TO MAKE IT TO THE SUBWAY. PROBABLY FEWER DANGERS DOWN THERE, RELATIVELY SPEAKING.
GET TO THE FANTASTIC FOUR, OR HORIZON... SOMEWHERE WITH THE EQUIPMENT TO FIGURE OUT WHAT CAUSED THIS, AND HOPEFULLY FIX IT.
NNH...GETTING WORSE...
SHUT IT OUT, PETE! I KNOW EVERY WARNING BELL IN YOUR HEAD IS GOING OFF, BUT THERE'S NOTHING THERE. THERE'S NOTHING--
FFSSTTT
HGKK!
HAHAHAHAHA HAHAHA
F-FORGOT THE FIRST RULE OF MY LIFE. IT'S NOT PARANOIA...
...IF THEY'RE REALLY...OUT TO GET YOU...
TALK ABOUT WALKING RIGHT INTO IT!

OKAY. GOT AWAY FROM THE PEOPLE WHO KNOW ME. NOW IF I CAN JUST--
OH, NO...

NNNAAAAHH!
COLLISION
COLLISION
COLLISION
COLLISION
HUGE METAL KILLING MACHINE
COLLISI
UNSAFE SPEED
COLLISION
KNOWN CARCINOGEN
COLLISION

TAKE YOUR MEDS, PAL.
W-WISH IT WAS THAT SIMPLE...
THE WHOLE WORLD' A POTENTIAL THREAT H-HEAD...SPLITTING..
FILTHY

NO...IT'S TOO MUCH...TOO... NNHHH...
THE HECK WAS THAT ABOUT? SHE WAS TALKING TO SPIDER-MAN...
DID EVERYONE IN THE CITY SEE THAT, OR JUST US?

PETER. THAT MESSAGE WASN'T FOR--
WHERE DID HE GO?
'SCUSE ME, BABE. GOTTA TAKE THIS. WORK.
BZZT BZZT

OU WORK HERE.
MIND YOUR OWN BUSINESS, YOU NOSY LITTLE--
YEAH, BOSS.

I HAVE AN ASSIGNMENT FOR YOU. ABOUT LOCATING SPIDER-MAN...

FUNNY YOU SHOULD MENTION THAT.
I WAS GOING TO TELL YOU I'VE GOT IT COVERED...

SPIDER-MAN! YOU *MUST* LISTEN!
IT'S COMING FOR YOU. IT'S RIGHT BEHIND YOU. YOU CAN'T-- CAN'T IGNORE IT. FLASH OF GOLD...
MADAME WEB?!
ANNND IT JUST GOT WORSE.

THANKS, JULIA. BRIN *SPIDER-MAN* A PSYC WARNING IN A CROWD OFFICE *WHILE* I'M *PET PARKER!* BIG HELP
I KNOW YOU MEAN W BUT URGENT NEWS C NO, IF I STICK AROU MY SECRET IDENTITY *HISTORY.*

OH, BOY...
COULD STALL
TOXIC CHEMICALS
CAUTION, WET FLOOR

SHUT *UP*, SPIDER-SENSE! I *CAN'T* FALL DOWN THE STAIRS! *I STICK TO WALLS!*
HOLD IT TOGETHER, PETE. JUST MAKE IT TO THE STREET...WHERE NO ONE PAYS ATTENTION TO CRAZY PEOPLE...

NNNAAAAAAAAA!
THE--THE FUTURE! EVERY POINT IN THE FUTURE! I CAN SEE--
EVERYTHING!

SORRY.
I-IT WAS... HOT...
WELL, THIS COMPUTER'S EXPENSIVE. GIVE ME A HAND HERE, KLUTZ.
MY SPIDER-SENSE...IT'S GONE INTO OVERDRIVE.
PAPER CUT
STATIC SHOCK
HIGH FRUCTOSE CORN SYRUP
PUNCTURE WOUNDS
EVERY POTENTIAL THREAT'S JOLTING MY NERVOUS SYSTEM...NO MATTER HOW SMALL.
AND EVEN THOUGH I KNOW WHAT'S HAPPENING NOW, MY BODY'S IN TOTAL FIGHT-OR-FLIGHT MODE. GOTTA GET SOMEWHERE SAFE...
UM...I... BATHROOM.
LOOKS LIKE ORIZON LABS DESN'T DRUG TEST THEIR EMPLOYEES...
BEFORE THIS GETS ANY WORSE...
GERMS
TEXTING WHILE WALKING
ATE BURRITOS FOR LUNCH
GGNNNN...

LOOK OUT!
YOU OKAY?
I WAS UNTIL SOME LUNATIC KNOCKED ME DOWN.
WHAT THE WHAT, PETE?
THERE'S DANGER...WE ALMOST...
MY BAD, BROSEPH. ALMOST BUMPED YA THERE.
Y'DON'T GOTTA MAKE A FEDERAL CASE OUT OF IT...
SORRY. I'M JUST...EDGY, I GUESS. DIDN'T HAVE MY COFFEE THIS MORNING.
WELL, HERE. CAFFEINATE BEFORE SOMEONE GETS HURT.
THANKS. I--
NO!!
DUDE!

YOUR JAMMER HAS ALREADY PROVEN A FAILURE.
YES...BUT I LEARNED FROM MY MISTAKES. I'M ADJUSTING THE SETTINGS. BOOSTING THE SIGNAL SIGNIFICANTLY AND SUBTLY ALTERING THE FREQUENCY.
I HAVE THESE SET UP ALL OVER TOWN. THEY'RE PRIMED...JUST WAITING TO BE SWITCHED ON.

911, WHAT IS YOUR EMERGENCY?
THERE IS A WOMAN IN DIRE NEED OF MEDICAL ATTENTION OUTSIDE THE PORT AUTHORITY BUS TERMINAL.
WHAT'S YOUR RELATIONSHIP TO THE VICTIM?

I'M HER.

YOU REALIZE IF THIS IS SOME STALLING TACTIC, YOU'LL ONLY MAKE ME ANGRIER.
I-IT'LL WORK. I PROMISE.
PLEASE...
KLIK

Shadowland.
THE KINGPIN'S STRONGHOLD.
YOU'VE BEEN USEFUL TO ME, STONE. YOU BROUGHT ME THE SECRETS OF HORIZON LABS. AND YOU WERE HANDSOMELY REWARDED.
YOU'RE AN EDUCATED MAN. YOU UNDERSTAND EQUATIONS HAVE TWO SIDES. SO CONSIDER, FOR A MOMENT, WHAT HAPPENS WHEN YOU DISAPPOINT ME.
M-MR. FISK ≠GKK≠ WAIT! GIVE ME A CHANCE TO MAKE IT RIGHT!
I HAVE A WAY TO GET THE BRIEFCASE BACK FROM SPIDER-MAN...
...AND CRIPPLE HIM IN THE PROCESS!
Port Authority Bus Terminal.
BYE, SWEETIE. BE GOOD.
I LOVE YOU.
PORT A
86020
86020
I--I REALLY THOUGHT I'D GET MORE TIME.
WELL. NO SENSE COMPLAINING.
BETTER MAKE GOOD USE OF WHAT I HAVE LEFT.

...AND I DOUBT WE'VE GOT ANYTHING THAT'S GOING TO BUMP *THAT* OFF THE FRONT PAGE.

NORAH, THIS IS ACTION FOOTAGE OF *HOBGOBLIN* FIGHTING *SPIDER-MAN!*

THAT'S EYE CANDY, PHIL. GIVE IT TO THE INTERNS. I'M LOOKING INTO THE *MEATY* STUFF. THE *LEGACY OF NORMAN OSBORN.* AND I DON'T JUST MEAN THE GOBLIN CULT.

OSBORN'S IN A *COMA*, BUT MY SOURCES SAY HE HAD DIRT ON *ALL* THE POWER PLAYERS. I BET HIS FILES MAKE J. EDGAR HOOVER'S LOOK TAME. AND *I'M* GONNA FIND 'EM.

COMPARED TO THAT, MAN O'MINE, THE HOBGOBLIN'S SMALL TIME.
I'M WHAT?! YOU LITTLE CLIMBER! YOU MADE YOUR NAME OFF OF COVERING THE HOBGOBLIN! AND NOW I'M "SMALL TIME"?!
HEY, LOOK WHO'S HERE! PETE!

AVEN'T SEEN YOU H SINCE YOU WENT SIT AT THE NERD'S TABLE. HOW'VE YOU BEEN?
NORAH'S BEEN COVERING THE PUNISHER...IS SHE IN TROUBLE?
Y'KNOW. MORE SCIENCE, MORE PROBLEMS.
I'VE GOTTA TALK SENSE INTO ROBBIE-- BUT IF SHE'S IN DANGER, I CAN'T BLOW HER OFF.

PETE, ARE YOU OKAY? YOU LOOK KINDA GREEN.
SO WHAT? YOU'RE MY GIRL! NOW YOU'RE INTO PARKER AGAIN?! MAYBE IT'S TIME HE "DISAPPEARED" FOR A WHILE...
NGH! JUST A HEADACHE... BUT IT IS GETTING WORSE.

"...GO TO THE TOP."
DAILY
BUGLE

ROBBIE, PLEASE, YOU CAN'T RUN IT!
PLEASE.
PLEASE.
PLEASE.
PLEASE.
I CAN'T NOT RUN IT...IT'S TRUE, AND IT'S NEWS. HAVE YOU READ THE ARTICLE? I THINK IT CASTS YOU AND HORIZON IN A VERY POSITIVE LIGHT.
BUT--BUT IF WORD GETS OUT I'M ASSOCIATED WITH SPIDER-MAN--

YOU'VE BEEN ASSOCIATED WITH SPIDER-MAN FOR YEARS. YOU RELEASED A BOOK OF PHOTOGRAPHS OF HIM. HOW IS THIS ANY DIFFERENT?
BECAUSE-- BECAUSE--
BECAUSE LIKE AN IDIOT I REVEALED MY SECRET IDENTITY TO THE WORLD...
...AND GOT DOCTOR STRANGE TO CAST A SPELL TO COVER IT BACK UP. BUT IF PEOPLE LOOK TOO CLOSELY IT COULD UNRAVEL AND--OY.

LOOK, JUST DELAY IT. GIVE ME SOME TIME TO...Y'KNOW, PREPARE.
WHY? YOU DON'T GO TO PRESS UNTIL TONIGHT!
PETER, IT'S THE TWENTY-FIRST CENTURY.
IT'S TOO LATE FOR THAT.

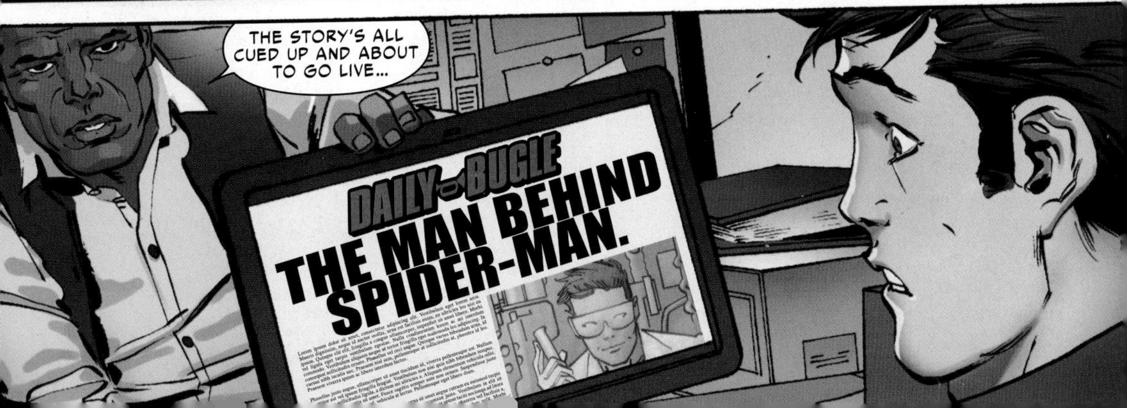
THE STORY'S ALL CUED UP AND ABOUT TO GO LIVE...
DAILY BUGLE
THE MAN BEHIND SPIDER-MAN.

Horizon Labs.
SOUTH STREET SEAPORT. MANHATTAN.
I'M DYING TO KNOW WHAT'S SO IMPORTANT THE GOBLIN CULT, HOBGOBLIN AND THE KINGPIN ARE ALL HOT TO GET THEIR HANDS ON THIS BRIEFCASE...
...BUT IT IS OBVIOUSLY BOOBY-TRAPPED, AND BEFORE I CAN PUT IN THE TIME TO CRACK IT, I'VE GOT TO FIND OUT IF TIBERIUS IS HERE, OR--
SLOW DOWN, PETE. JUST 'CAUSE YOU DON'T LIKE THE GUY DOESN'T MEAN HE'S WORKING WITH HOBGOBLIN. YOU'RE A SCIENTIST. SUPPORT YOUR HYPOTHESIS WITH FACTS.
THERE. IT'LL BE SAFE IN MY SPIDEY-VAULT WHILE I SHAKE THE RUST OFF MY JOURNALISM SKILLS. I STILL REMEMBER LESSON ONE: FOR ANSWERS, YOU GO TO THE TOP.
HEY, MAX, HAVE YOU SEEN-- OH, SORRY.
NOT AT ALL, COME IN. PETER, DO YOU KNOW SALLY FLOYD? SHE'S DOING A PROFILE ON US FOR THE DAILY BUGLE.
I HOPE YOU'LL GIVE HER A MINUTE. WITH ALL THE PRESSURE MAYOR JAMESON'S BEEN PUTTING ON US LATELY, WE COULD STAND SOME GOOD PRESS.
SURE, I REMEMBER SALLY...FROM THE OLD BUGLE. SEEING YOU MAKES ME ALL KINDS OF NOSTALGIC.
YOU'VE COME A LONG WAY SINCE THEN. FREELANCE SHUTTERBUG TO BIG-TIME RESEARCHER...AND THE GUY WHO DESIGNS TECH FOR SPIDER-MAN.
WHAT? YOU'RE, UH, YOU'RE NOT PUTTING THAT IN THE ARTICLE, ARE YOU?
SORRY, PETER. LOOKS LIKE SOME OF OUR STAFF SPOKE OUT OF TURN. MS. FLOYD, I'M GOING TO HAVE TO ASK YOU TO REMOVE--
NO CAN DO, MR. MODELL. LOOK, PETE, I'M NOT TRYING TO MAKE YOUR LIFE DIFFICULT, BUT THIS IS GOLD...AND ON THE RECORD. YOU WANT THE STORY KILLED, YOU'RE GONNA HAVE TO REMEMBER THE OLD REPORTER'S RULE...

Astoria, Queens.

HOME TO JULIA CARPENTER, THE MYSTERIOUS MADAME WEB.

MY PSYCHIC WEB UNRAVELS. THE FUTURE SLIPS THROUGH MY FINGERS LIKE GOSSAMER.

AN *ENDING* APPROACHES...

NOK NOK

MOM? IT'S TIME. BUS LEAVES IN AN HOUR.

CAN I JUST SAY ONE MORE TIME HOW MUCH I *HATE* STAYING IN COLORADO? EVERYONE IN THAT TOWN IS AS *ANCIENT* AS GRANDMA AND GRANDPA.

THAT'S WHY IT'S IMPORTANT TO SPEND TIME WITH THEM, RACHEL. THE PEOPLE YOU LOVE... WON'T BE AROUND FOREVER.

MOM! THEY'RE, LIKE, SIXTY. DON'T BE SUCH A DOWNER. ANYWAY, I DON'T SEE *YOU* PACKING FOR AN EXTENDED STAY IN THE NAP CAPITAL OF THE WORLD.

IT'S NOT THAT I DON'T *WANT* TO BE WITH YOU, HONEY. BUT I...HAVE A LOT TO DO.

JUST REMEMBER HOW MUCH I LOVE YOU. AND THAT PART OF ME WILL ALWAYS BE WITH YOU.

UM, Y'KNOW, THERE'S THIS INVENTION CALLED ***SKYPE.*** YOU CAN TALK TO PEOPLE WHO ARE FAR AWAY. IT'S LIKE A TELEPHONE, BUT WITH ***PICTURES.***

GO EASY ON THE OLD FOLKS, KIDDO. THEY'RE DOING THEIR BEST.

AND SO HAVE I. WHATEVER'S COMING, YOU'LL BE SAFE WHEN IT HITS...AND TAKEN CARE OF AFTER I'M GONE.

WHICH COULD BE ANY DAY NOW. BECAUSE IT' BECOME CLEAR TO ME THAT THE END COMING IS MINE.

BINGO. YOUR BAT-DRONE'S GPS LED ME RIGHT TO YOU.
IDIOT! I BET YOU DON'T EVEN KNOW IT'S GOT GPS. AND WHY WOULD YOU?
YOU STOLE IT FROM OSBORN MONTHS AGO.
I HAD IT FOR YEARS. NO ONE KNOWS THAT TECH BETTER THAN ME. NO ONE!
AND THAT'S HOW THE REAL HOBGOBLIN IS GOING TO MAKE YOU PAY!
HEH HEH HEH
SO MUCH TO SEE...AND SO LITTLE TIME.

DAMN DAMN DAMN! KILL HIM!
WHILE I GET THE HE OUT OF HERE.

STONE, YOU MORON! YOU SAID THIS THING WOULD FRY HIS SPIDER-SENSE! YOU JACKED IT INTO OVERDRIVE!
I'M GONNA DROP YOU RIGHT ON YOUR UGLY--
WAIT! I CAN FIX IT! I HAVE ALL THE DATA I NEED NOW. WITH A FEW MINOR ADJUSTMENTS, I CAN MAKE IT WORK NEXT TIME!

GREAT. BEAUTIFUL. JUST ONE THING STANDING BETWEEN YOU AND EMPLOYEE OF THE MONTH: SPIDER-MAN HAS THE CASE! HOW DO I EXPLAIN THAT TO THE KINGPIN?
HOLD ON. I'M NOT GONNA EXPLAIN IT TO HIM.
YOU ARE.
BUY-W

HUH. COULD'VE SWORN I SAW...
NO, I'M CERTAIN OF IT. THAT WAS TIBERIUS STONE FROM HORIZON LABS UP THERE!
I HAVE TO CHECK THIS OUT. AND I KNOW JUST WHERE TO START...
BIFF COLA

IF BY "DONE" YOU MEAN "COOKED TO PERFECTION," YOU WERE DEAD ON, HOBBY. I'M IN THE ZONE HERE!
HOA! WHAT JUST HAPPENED? MY PIDER-SENSE IS FIRING ON ALL YLINDERS TONIGHT.
OBODY'S LAYING A FINGER ON ME. NOT THAT I'M OMPLAINING. AFTER YEARS OF PARKER LUCK...
'M MORE THAN APPY TO TAKE E OCCASIONAL GIFT HORSE.
MAN, DR. OZ WASN'T KIDDING ABOUT A GOOD NIGHT'S SLEEP MAKING ALL THE DIFFERENCE.
What
DANGER ZONE
ART ONE: WARNING SIGNS
AN SLOTT & RISTOS GAGE
WRITERS
GIUSEPPE CAMUNCOLI
PENCILS
DAN GREEN
INKS
ANTONIO FABELA
COLORS
VC'S CHRIS ELIOPOULOS
LETTERER
STEVE McNIVEN
COVER
E PYLE
ANT EDITOR
STEPHEN WACKER
EDITOR
AXEL ALONSO
EDITOR IN CHIEF
JOE QUESADA
CHIEF CREATIVE OFFICER
DAN BUCKLEY
PUBLISHER
ALAN FINE
EXEC. PRODUCER

...BUT I STILL GOTTA *LAUGH.*

HAHAHAHAHAHAHAHA

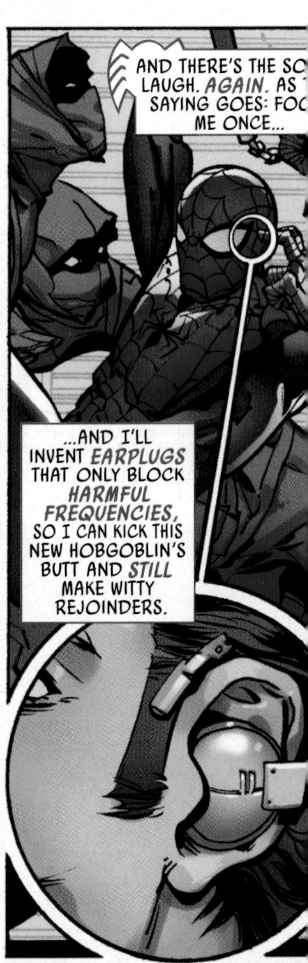

AND THERE'S THE SC LAUGH. *AGAIN.* AS T SAYING GOES: FOO ME ONCE...
...AND I'LL INVENT *EARPLUGS* THAT ONLY BLOCK *HARMFUL FREQUENCIES,* SO I CAN KICK THIS NEW HOBGOBLIN'S BUTT AND *STILL* MAKE WITTY REJOINDERS.

LAUGH TRACKS ARE PASSÉ, HOBBY. LET THE MATERIAL SPEAK FOR ITSELF.
THINK YOU'RE SMART 'CAUSE YOU FOUND A NEW TRICK? WELL, GUESS WHAT... SO DID I.
YOU'RE *DONE,* PUNK. B TEAM...

...GO!

Brooklyn.
A BIKER BAR NEAR THE EAST RIVER.
BROOKLYN
WHOK
I HOPE YOU GOBLIN GANGERS LEARNED A VALUABLE LESSON TODAY. GETTING TATTOOS OF NORMAN OSBORN DOESN'T MAKE YOU TOUGH, JUST STUPID.
STUPID AND LUCKY. 'CAUSE I GOT A SOFT SPOT FOR DUDES WHO'D INK A GOBLIN FACE ON THEIR SKIN...
EVEN IF IT IS THE WRONG GOBLIN. HAHAHAHAHA!
BESIDES, YOU GUYS JUST MADE ME RICH. YOUR LITTLE PULP FICTION BRIEFCASE IS GONNA PUT THE KINGPIN IN A VERY GENEROUS MOOD...
CAN'T HAVE THAT.
SNAP
HELL YELLERS
THE "JOLLY FAT GUY" GIMMICK IS SANTA'S TRADEMARK. AND HE'S VERY LITIGIOUS.
BIFF COLA
SPIDER-MAN! Y'KNOW, NEW YORK HAS STALKER LAWS. THE WAY YOU'VE BEEN DOGGING ME, I OUGHTA CALL THE COPS.
I DO LIKE HEARING YOUR JOKES, THOUGH. THEY'RE NEVER FUNNY...

AMAZING SPIDER-MAN #695
COVER BY STEVE MCNIVEN

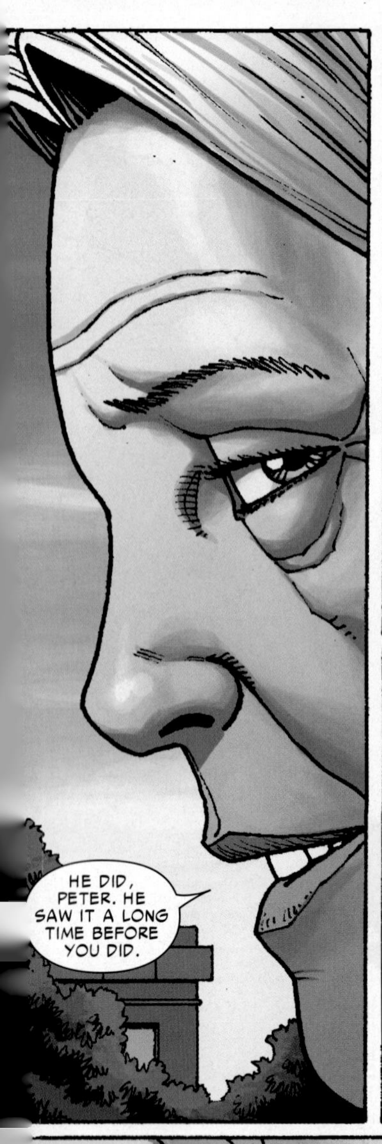
HE DID, PETER. HE SAW IT A LONG TIME BEFORE YOU DID.

NOW, LET'S LET HIM GET SOME REST.

BEN PARKER

R.I.P.

R.I.P.

WHY ON EARTH DO YOU THINK THAT WOULD MAKE ONE BIT OF DIFFERENCE?

YOU THINK HE'D CARE?

I JUST... I JUST WISH HE COULD HAVE SEEN WHAT BECAME OF ME.

AND SO DOES HE.

NOW, LET'S GET GOING, SHALL WE?

KER
BEN PARKER
R.I.P.

IT *WAS* MY FAULT THOUGH.

"UNTIL NOW YOU HAVEN'T HAD TO BE."

I SAID ALL THAT?
I THINK SO. THAT'S HOW I REMEMBER IT, AT LEAST.

WELL, THEN. MAYBE I DO DESERVE A SCHOLARSHIP.
OR AT LEAST LUNCH. ARE YOU HUNGRY, PETER? WE COULD--
WAIT.

I...I WANT YOU TO KNOW THAT I DO...YOU KNOW...
I DO HELP PEOPLE.
I KNOW I'VE SEEN...

NO, I MEAN...I KNOW I COME OFF AS A BIT OF A SCREW-UP, BUT I WANT YOU TO KNOW...
I MEAN, ALL THAT STUFF YOU SAID I'D DO...I...
...I THINK BEN WOULD...
PETER.
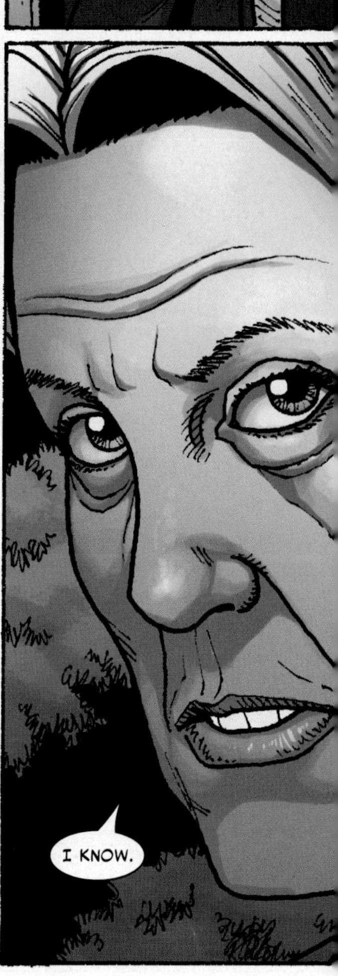
I KNOW.

AND YOU'LL FEEL WEAK WHERE BEN'S STRENGTH USED TO PROP YOU UP.
BUT YOU'LL HONOR HIM BY STANDING ON YOUR OWN.
BECAUSE YOU'LL SEE THAT BEN TAUGHT YOU HOW TO BE *STRONG*, AND YOU'LL SHOW THE WORLD THAT HIS *STRENGTH* STILL SUSTAINS YOU.
YOU'RE GOING TO HELP PEOPLE, PETER. I KNOW YOU ARE. BECAUSE BEN WOULD.
HOW DO YOU KNOW, PETER?
YOU WON'T LISTEN TO ME. I'M NOTHING LIKE UNCLE BEN.
UNTIL NOW...

"YOU'LL SEE THAT LIFE IS TEMPORARY.
"FRAGILE.
"THAT EVERY DEATH IS AS IMPORTANT TO SOMEONE AS BEN'S WAS TO YOU...
"...THAT EVERY LIFE IS WORTH PROTECTING."

AM...AM I ALWAYS GOING TO FEEL THIS WAY?
YOU'RE WOUNDED, PETER. IT'S A WOUND THAT STAYS WITH YOU. CHANGES YOU.
"YOU'LL SEE THE PAIN OF THIS WORLD MORE READILY. YOU KNOW IT'S THERE NOW.
"YOU WON'T BE ABLE TO IGNORE IT.

PETER.

IT'S TIME TO GET UP.

IT WAS MY FAULT, AUNT--
NO MORE OF THAT.

THIS THING WE'VE BEEN ASKED TO BEAR...AS *UNNATURAL* AND *WRONG* AS IT FEELS... IT'S A PART OF LIFE. IT'S *NORMAL*.
THAT MAY BE THE HARDEST PART.
IT'S TIME TO GET UP, PETER.

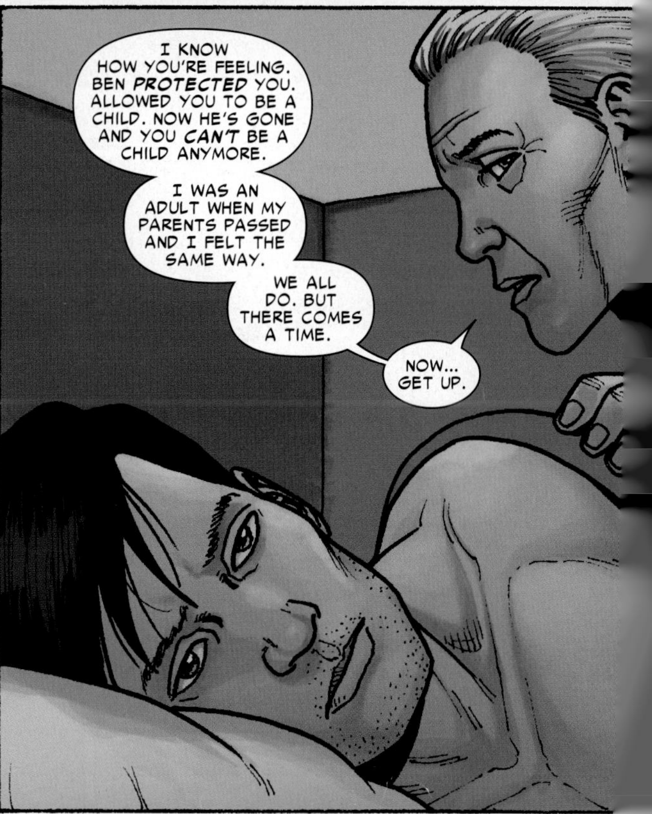
I KNOW HOW YOU'RE FEELING. BEN *PROTECTED* YOU. ALLOWED YOU TO BE A CHILD. NOW HE'S GONE AND YOU *CAN'T* BE A CHILD ANYMORE.
I WAS AN ADULT WHEN MY PARENTS PASSED AND I FELT THE SAME WAY.
WE ALL DO. BUT THERE COMES A TIME.
NOW... GET UP.

IT'S FUNNY, ISN'T IT?
WHAT'S THAT?
HOW WHEN HE DIED IT FELT LIKE THE WORLD HAD ENDED. HOW NOTHING WOULD EVER BE NORMAL AGAIN. HOW THE JOY HAD LEFT US.
BUT IT'S BEEN ALL THESE YEARS...AND HERE WE ARE. TALKING. SMILING.
THE WORLD KEPT SPINNING.

OF COURSE, YOUR WORLD SPINS AN HOUR OR TWO BEHIND EVERYONE ELSE'S, BUT STILL...
OH, YEAH... SORRY I WAS LATE.
THAT'S OKAY, PETER. IT'S FUN TO TEASE YOU.

IT MUST HAVE BEEN HARD ON YOU. I KNEW HOW TO NURTURE YOU, BUT BEN WAS YOUR STRENGTH.

NOW WHO'S BEING FUNNY?
AUNT MAY, YOU WERE MY "MOTHER." YOU KNOW FULL WELL--

--I WOULD NEVER HAVE MADE IT WITHOUT YOU.

YOUR AUNT HAD A LOT OF GOOD THINGS TO SAY TODAY, PETER...
TH- THANKS, MISTER WEISS.
I HAVEN'T SEEN HER FOR A WHILE. MAYBE YOU SHOULD GO CHECK ON HER.

AUNT MAY?

I'M A LIAR, PETER...
A TERRIBLE, TERRIBLE LIAR.

I'D GIVE ANYTHING FOR JUST ONE MORE MOMENT.
ANYTHING...

IT'S NORMAL, WHEN WE LOSE SOMEONE WE LOVE, TO SAY THAT WE WOULD GIVE ANYTHING TO SEE THEM FOR JUST ONE MORE MOMENT.
THAT *ONE MORE MOMENT* WOULD BE ENOUGH.
TODAY
MEMORIAL SERVICES FOR BENJAMIN PARKER
I CAN'T SAY THAT.
IF I HAD ONE MORE MOMENT I'D JUST WANT ANOTHER.
THEN ANOTHER.
THE TRUTH IS WHEN YOU *LOVE* SOMEONE LIKE I LOVED BEN...
ONLY ONE MORE MOMENT WOULD BE...TOO PAINFUL TO BEAR...

I THOUGHT NOW WOULD BE A GOOD TIME TO TELL YOU... I KNOW BEN ALWAYS SAID EDUCATION WAS THE MOST IMPORTANT THING, SO I'M STARTING A SCHOLARSHIP. IN HIS NAME.
"THE BENJAMIN PARKER SCIENCE GRANT."
WITH HORIZON LAB'S HELP, IT WILL--
PSSHAW-- HA!

WHAT?
"THE BEN PARKER--" HAHA! I'M SORRY, BUT A SCIENCE GRANT? IF YOU PUT YOUR EAR TO THE GROUND YOU CAN PROBABLY HEAR BEN SPINNING IN HIS GRAVE.
WHAT?! YOU ALWAYS TOLD ME BEN THOUGHT EVERYONE SHOULD GO TO COLLEGE!
BECAUSE I WANTED YOU TO GO. PETER, ONE OF BEN'S PROUDEST MOMENTS WAS BARELY GRADUATING HIGH SCHOOL.

SCIENCE GRANT. THAT'S RICH.
BUT HE BOUGHT ME THAT MICROSCOPE...
UNDER DURESS. IF I HADN'T THROWN A FIT HE WOULD HAVE BROUGHT HOME ANOTHER BASEBALL MITT "JUST TO SEE IF IT'D TAKE."
IF YOU REALLY WANT TO HONOR BEN, YOU SHOULD BUY SOME SMART, YOUNG STUDENT SEASON TICKETS FOR THE METS.

UH-OH, I KNOW THAT LOOK...
HE'S GETTING A SCHOLARSHIP.
AND HE'D REALLY BE TOUCHED ABOUT IT.
SAYS YOU.
ABSOLUTELY "SAYS ME."
KEEP IT UP AND I'M GIVING YOU ONE, TOO.

PETER PARKER, DON'T YOU DARE. YOU KNOW I DON'T DO WELL IN THE SPOTLIGHT.

YOU HAVE TO TRY AND GO TO SCHOOL TODAY, SWEETHEART.
BEN WOULDN'T WANT YOU MISSING SCHOOL.

DOES IT GO AWAY?

WHAT?
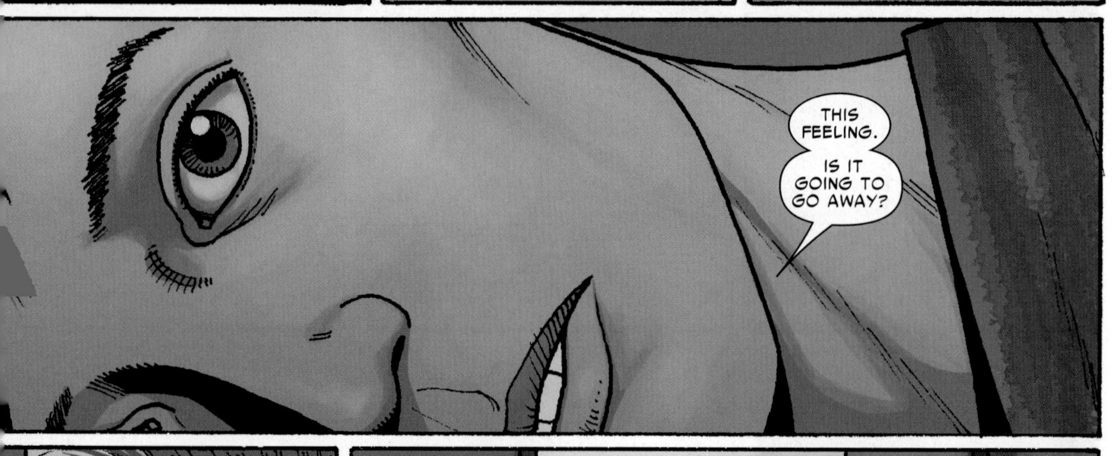
THIS FEELING.
IS IT GOING TO GO AWAY?
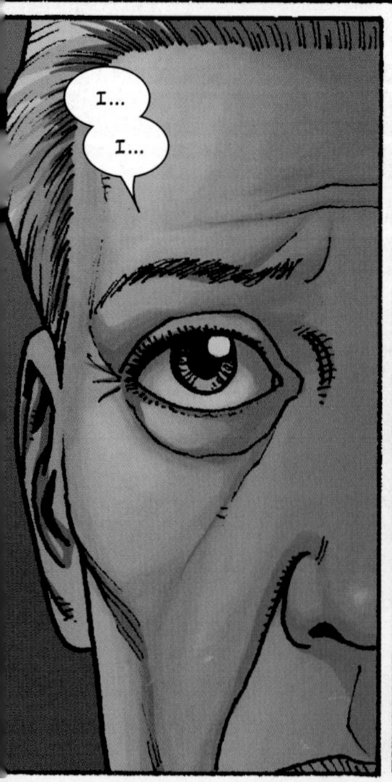
I...
I...

BEN WOULDN'T WANT YOU MISSING SCHOOL.

MISSED YOU.
YOU TOO.

HOW'S JAY?
OH, STOP. NOT IN FRONT OF BEN...

COME ON, AUNT MAY. HE'D WANT YOU TO BE HAPPY.
I KNOW... HE WOULD. BUT WE MADE YOUTHFUL PROMISES TO EACH OTHER. LIKE ALL KIDS DO.
THERE'S JUST NO NEED TO THROW IT IN HIS FACE.

YOU DON'T THINK HE'S UP THERE WATCHING US ALL THE TIME, DO YOU? I'D HATE TO THINK HE'D SEE ME AND JAY--
UH, YOU'RE RIGHT. LET'S NOT TALK ABOUT THIS HERE.
I MEAN, I THOUGHT THAT PART OF MY LIFE WAS OVER, BUT--
SAY NO MORE. GOT IT.
SOMETIMES I'D SWEAR JAY'S REALLY A 25-YEAR-OLD--
AUNT MAY--

GOT. IT.

OH, PETER. ALWAYS SUCH A SENSITIVE BOY...

hen.
DIDN'T YOU HEAR ME, PETER?! I TOLD YOU TO STAY IN YOUR ROOM!
YOU FOLLOWED THE POLICE, DIDN'T YOU?

ARE YOU OKAY, PETER? DID THEY CATCH HIM? DID--

IT... IT WAS *ME*.
IT WAS MY FAULT.

OH, PETER...

I'LL HEAR NONE OF THAT...

I KNOW...

I KNOW...
I KNOW...
I KNOW...

YOU SAY THAT EVERY YEAR.
AND YOU NEVER LET ME EXPLAIN.

THAT'S BECAUSE THE IDEA IS SO PROFOUNDLY STUPID.

HEH. SAYS YOU.
ABSOLUTELY "SAYS ME."

IT WAS MY FAULT, YOU KNOW.
PARKER
BEN PARKER
R.I.P.
R.I.P.

Queens, New York.
YEP, AN HOUR LATE, ON THE DOT.
I TOLD YOU WE SHOULD'VE LEFT AT NOON.
THIS IS MY NEPHEW WE'RE TALKING ABOUT, JAY. WHY WOULD WE POSSIBLY WANT TO GET HERE ON TIME?
AN HOUR LATE IS JUST ABOUT PERFECT.
BUT YOU'RE SURE HE'S COMING?
DON'T BE SILLY, HONEY.
HE'LL BE HERE.
I'LL BE BACK IN AN HOUR.
THANK YOU.
PARKER

GARK--
RACK
WHOA-- WAIT A MINUTE!
NO ONE THROWS COPPERHEAD!
--ARCK!
HEY, LADY!
CALL THE COPS. I'M LATE.
THWIP
NOT ONE ZING?
HE WAS IN A HURRY.
I THOUGHT WE'D AT LEAST GET A ONE-LINER ON HIS WAY OUT...I MEAN, AM I CRAZY OR DID HE PHONE THAT ONE IN?
NO...
IT WAS WEIRD.

New York City.
THE GUY RUNNING AWAY IS COPPERHEAD, MEMBER OF THE VILLAINOUS SERPENT SOCIETY.
STOP!

DUKE, STOP HIM!
ARE YOU CRAZY?! THAT'S--
LOOK, HIS NAME ESCAPES ME, BUT STILL--

PUT IT DOWN.

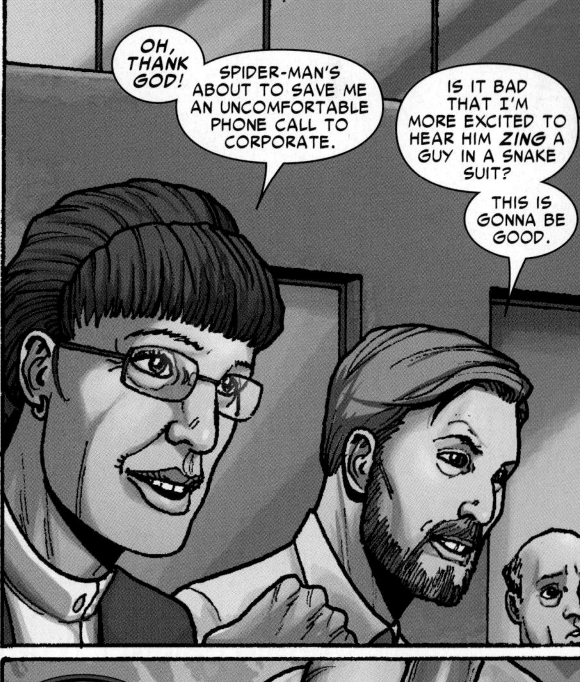
OH, THANK GOD!
SPIDER-MAN'S ABOUT TO SAVE ME AN UNCOMFORTABLE PHONE CALL TO CORPORATE.
IS IT BAD THAT I'M MORE EXCITED TO HEAR HIM ZING A GUY IN A SNAKE SUIT?
THIS IS GONNA BE GOOD.

SPIDER-MAN...
...I HOPE YOU APPRECIATE WHAT A MASSIVE MISTAKE IT WAS TO MAKE ENEMIES OF THE SERPENT SOCIE--

AVENGING
SPIDER-MAN

PREVIOUSLY...

AS YOU MAY HAVE GATHERED, PETER PARKER WAS FAR FROM BEING THE BIGGEST MAN ON CAMPUS! BUT, HIS UNCLE BEN THOUGHT HE WAS A PRETTY SPECIAL LAD...
YOU'RE NOT FOOLIN' ME, PETEY! I KNOW YOU'RE AWAKE -- AND IT'S TIME FOR SCHOOL!
GOSH, UNCLE BEN--YOU'RE WORSE THAN A ROOM FULL OF ALARM CLOCKS!

AS FOR PETE'S AUNT MAY, SHE THOUGHT THE SUN ROSE AND SET UPON HER NEPHEW!
I COOKED YOUR FAVORITE BREAKFAST, PETEY--WHEATCAKES!
DON'T FATTEN HIM UP TOO MUCH, DEAR! I CAN HARDLY OUT-WRESTLE HIM NOW!

WRITER: **ZEB WELLS** ARTIST: **STEVE DILLON**

OLORS: **FRANK MARTIN JR.** LETTERER: **VC's JOE CARAMAGNA**

COVER: **CHRIS SAMNEE & JAVIER RODRIGUEZ**

SISTANT EDITOR: **ELLIE PYLE** ASSOCIATE EDITOR: **SANA AMANAT** SENIOR EDITOR: **STEPHEN WACKER**

EXECUTIVE EDITOR: **TOM BREVOORT** EDITOR IN CHIEF: **AXEL ALONSO**

CHIEF CREATIVE OFFICER: **JOE QUESADA** PUBLISHER: **DAN BUCKLEY** EXECUTIVE PRODUCER: **ALAN FINE**

FIFTY YEARS AGO **STAN LEE** AND **STEVE DITKO** GAVE THE WORLD SPIDER-MAN. WE THANK THEM AND DEDICATE THIS ISSUE TO THEIR LEGACY.

AVENGING SPIDER-MAN #11

"...NO MATTER WHAT COMES ALONG."
DELVADIA
HM. NEW YORK AIR.
NO, THAT'S NOT DOING IT FOR ME.
WHERE ID I LEAVE IT...?
THERE WE GO.
NOW.
NOW I'M HOME.
Next: HOBGOBLIN

I'M SORRY, BUT AS I EXPLAINED TO YOUR AUNT AND HER HUSBAND...
...THOUGH, IN TIME, SHE'LL BE ABLE TO WALK WITH A *CANE*, SHE'LL NEVER HAVE FULL USE OF THE LEG AGAIN.
IS THERE ANY KIND OF PROCEDURE OR OPERATION?
I'D RATHER NOT, IF WE DON'T HAVE TO. YOUR AUNT IS VERY OLD--
BOYS, I'M *RIGHT* HERE. AND MY *HEARING* IS EXCELLENT.
NOW WHEN IT COMES TO PHYSICAL THERAPY, SHE'LL NEED LOTS OF HELP FROM *FRIENDS* AND *FAMILY.*
I CAN RECOMMEND A NUMBER OF PLACES IN BOSTON--
NO.
SHE HAS ALL THE FRIENDS AND FAMILY SHE NEEDS...
...RIGHT *HERE*.
WELL, I KNOW SHE'D LIKE THAT...
AND YOUR *SON* WOULD TOO. TRUST ME.
I DO MISS IT HERE. BUT JAY, ARE YOU SURE?
YOU ALWAYS THOUGHT NEW YORK WAS TOO DANGEROUS *BEFORE.* AND *NOW* LOOK AT US.
WELL, I THINK THE *BEST* PLACE FOR YOU GUYS IS WHERE *I* CAN KEEP AN EYE OUT FOR YOU...

"YOUR ALPHA
DAYS ARE A THING
OF THE PAST.
"NO MORE COMMERCIALS,
PRESS TOURS, OR TV SPOTS.
"SAY GOODBYE TO
THE PENTHOUSE..."
WELCOME
HOME, SON.
"...AND THAT'S
IT FOR PRIVATE
TUTORS.
"IT'S BACK
TO MIDTOWN
HIGH....
"...WHERE YOU
WON'T BE A NOBODY
ANYMORE.
"YOU'LL BE THE
KID WHO USED
TO BE SOMEBODY.
"AND IT'LL
STING FOR
A WHILE.
EVERYONE'LL HAVE
A GOOD LAUGH.
UT EVENTUALLY,
HEY'LL FORGET.
EVERYONE WILL.
"EVEN GUYS
LIKE THE JACKAL.
"BUT YOU'LL
KNOW.
"AND I'LL
KNOW...
"...THAT A LITTLE
BIT OF THAT POWER'S
IN YOU. ALWAYS THERE.
AND GROWING.
"AND MAYBE,
WE'LL TRY THIS
AGAIN SOMEDAY.
"WITH A MASK.
AND DEFINITELY
NOT AS ALPHA.
"THAT'S
OVER."

"...I'LL PUT IT TO GOOD USE."
SO? YOU FINALLY COMING IN TODAY, ANDY?
YEAH, YEAH. BUT THINK WE CAN HURRY THIS UP, PARKER?
I GOT A TABLE READING AT TEN. I'M GUEST-STARRING ON VAMPIRE DIARIES.
HUH? SPIDEY? THOUGHT I WAS TALKING TO PARKER.
NOPE. PETE COULDN'T MAKE IT. I'M FILLING IN.
YOU CAN DO THAT? WORK THE TECH AND ALL?
WHAT CAN I SAY? I'M A SPIDER-MAN OF MANY TALENTS.
STEP RIGHT UP.
WAIT, SOMETHING'S OFF. THIS MONITOR-THING LOOKS DIFFERENT...
I MADE SOME ALTERATIONS.
WHAT KIND OF--?
YOU'LL SEE. AND REMEMBER, PETER AND HORIZON HAD NOTHING TO DO WITH THIS. THIS IS ALL ME.
HEY, I FEEL...
ALPHA-POWERED DOWN.
I CAN'T TAKE ALL OF IT OUT OF YOU, BUT I CAN DRAIN MOST OF IT AWAY.
BUT WHY WOULD YOU--?
BECAUSE YESTERDAY WAS A TEST. AND YOU FAILED. YOU USED YOUR POWER IRRESPONSIBLY.

...HE WILL BE STOPPED."
SO? WHAT DO WE DO WITH THIS BIG GUY? CAN'T EXACTLY LOCK 'IM UP IN THE RAFT.
IT TOOK SOME DOING, CAPTAIN, BUT THE DAY IS OURS!
THANKS, IN NO SMALL PART TO ALPHA, BUT AT WHAT COST?
AND I SEE HE'S TAKEN OFF AGAIN.
AYE. A MOST CHURLISH YOUTH.
THE NEGATIVE ZONE? MAYBE SET UP A CONTAINMENT CELL ON MONSTER ISAND?
ONE THING'S FOR SURE...
...TERMINUS'S ENERGY LANCE IS GETTING SHIPPED STRAIGHT TO PROJECT: PEGASUS--
NO!
SPIDER-MAN?
WHAT ON EARTH FOR, SON?
I NEED IT.
THAT DIDN'T JUST DEFLECT ALPHA'S ENERGY...
...IT REDIRECTED IT.
YOU LET ME STUDY THAT ALIEN TECH...
...FIGURE OUT HOW IT WORKS, AND I PROMISE YOU...

ALL EMERGENCY VEHICLES TO RUNWAY FOUR.
DIVERT ALL INCOMING FLIGHTS.
RUNWAY FOUR IS NOW CLOSED.
REPEAT. ALL VEHICLES TO RUNWAY FOUR.
GOOD GOD! SPIDER-MAN, ARE YOU--?
DON'T WORRY ABOUT ME. THERE'RE TWO PASSENGERS ON BOARD.
WE GOT 'EM, SON. NOW LET US HAVE A LOOK AT--
OUT OF THE WAY, DAGBLASTIT! MAYOR COMING THROUGH! LISTEN UP, WALL-CRAWLER--
ARE YOU FOR REAL, J.J.? I JUST LANDED A SMALL JET ON MY BACK!
WHATEVER YOU HAVE TO SAY--
THANK YOU.
WHA?
I'M NOT AN IDIOT. YOU DID IT AGAIN. YOU SAVED MY FAMILY.
MY FATHER AND HIS WIFE WERE ON THAT PLANE. AND THANKS TO YOU--
THEY'RE GONNA BE ALL RIGHT?
THE WOMAN, MAY PARKER, YOU KNOW HER.
PETER'S AUNT.
HER LEG WA INJURED IN TH LANDING. DON WORRY. I'M GETTING HE THE BEST CA IN THE CITY
NOW TELL ME, WHO W RESPONSIB FOR ALL O THIS?
A TEENAGER. A MENACE. AND I SWEAR TO YOU, JONAH...

JAY, I...
I LOVE YOU TOO, HONEY.
MALL PRIVATE JET. AT ARE WE TALKING ABOUT HERE?
ANDING WEIGHT, VER SEVENTY-FIVE OUSAND POUNDS.
IT'S FULL ON FUEL, DD ANOTHER THIRTY D FORTY THOUSAND. N THERE'S THE THRUST--
NO. DON'T THINK.
JUST DO! C'MON, PARKER!
RGHHH!
CRRE CHKK

WE *CAN'T* STAY UP HERE. WE HAVE TO BRING HER IN.
AGREED.
BUT LOOK--I'M GETTING A WARNING LIGHT ON THE LANDING GEAR.
BOTH OF YOU, STAY STRAPPED IN!
I'LL CHECK IT OUT.
WHAT DO YOU SEE?
GRNHH!
ENOUGH HERE FOR EIGHT WEB-PARACHUTES.
SPIDER-MAN?!
GIMME A SEC!
RIP
YEP.
WE'RE AMAZINGLY, SPECTACULARLY AND SENSATIONALLY SCREWED.
RUNWAY'S CLEAR! I'M GONNA GO FOR IT.
LANDING GEAR DOWN?
IT WILL BE!
I PROMISE.
AN ENTIRE STRUT'S MISSING FROM THE ASSEMBLY...
...AND THERE'S ONLY *ONE* THING I CAN USE AS A REPLACEMENT PART...
SPIDER-SENSE IS TELLING ME THIS'S *INCREDIBLY* DANGEROUS.
NO DOY.

...YOU LET THE GUY WITH SPIDER-SENSE DO THE DRIVING.
PLEASE PICK UP.
PETER?
PETER?
AW NO! AFTER MISSING TOO MANY OF HER CALLS...
...I SWITCHED MY EARPIECE TO ALWAYS PICK UP FOR...
IT'S AUNT MAY...
IT'S AUNT MAY...
...IN CASE SOMETHING HAPPENS, I WANT YOU TO KNOW...
...IN CASE SOMETHING HAPPENS, I WANT YOU TO KNOW...
...I HAVE ALWAYS LOVED YOU AS IF YOU WERE MY OWN--
...I HAVE ALWAYS LOVED YOU AS IF YOU WERE MY OWN--
MRS. PARKER-JAMESON!
SORRY.
KZOWW
IF YOU COULD PLEASE TURN OFF YOUR CELL PHONE.
BUT I--
F.A.A. REGULATIONS.
O-OKAY.
SPIDER-MAN!
WHAT NOW?!

...COULD GO HORRIBLY WRONG?!
I--I WILL NOT BE BESTED BY SOME CHILD!
BRAKKOW
CHILD? HEY, LOSER! I'M ALPHA!
THE BEST DAMN HERO THIS WORLD'S GOT!
ARROGANT SWAIN!
CEASE YOUR ATTACK!
THOR! GET HIM OUT OF HERE!
THE KID DOESN'T KNOW WHAT HE'S DOING!
FORGET TERMINUS--WE'VE GOT CIVILIANS UP HERE WITH US! ALPHA'S GOING TO GET US ALL KILLED!
HERE WE GO AGAIN. ALL SYSTEMS OFF.
THE PLANE CAN'T TAKE THIS--
SORRY, JAY...
...BUT WE DON'T HAVE A CHOICE!
AAAND WE'RE BACK. NOW WHAT DO YOU SAY I TAKE THE CONTROLS FROM HERE.
DO YOU KNOW HOW TO FLY?
ACTUALLY? NO. BUT I'VE SEEN IT A LOT.
TRUST ME, TIMES LIKE THIS...

HI. THIS YOUNG LADY WANTED TO VISIT THE COCKPIT.
SPIDER-MAN?! WHAT ARE YOU DOING HERE?
MAY? ARE YOU ALL RIGHT?
J-JUST A LITTLE SHAKEN, DEAR. I'LL BE FINE.
THANK GOD. NOW AS FOR YOU...
...ARE YOU WHY WE DEPRESSURIZED?
AH. YES. BUT...
...I'M ALSO THE GUY WHO'S GONNA GET US OUT OF HERE. SO IT EVENS OUT.
JUST DO WHAT I DO, JAY, AND WE'LL BE JUST FINE.
ALPHA-ENERGY SHORTED OUT YOUR SYSTEMS.
WE NEED TO SHUT EVERYTHING OFF...
...AND RESTART.
HOPE THIS WORKS...
YES!
SPIDER-MAN, YOU DID IT! WE'RE SAFE.
WHSHH
YUP. SAFELY IN THE MIDDLE OF EVIL, ALIEN SPACESHIPS. YAY, US. WONDER WHAT ELSE...

MRS. PARKER!
HOLD ON, I'VE GOT YOU!
IT--IT'S PARKER-JAMESON.
WHAT?
I GOT MARRIED.
FALLING OUT OF THE SKY AND THAT'S WHAT SHE'S WORRIED ABOUT.
WHAT?
NOTHING, MA'AM. YOU FOCUS ON WHATEVER YOU WANT...
...LEAVE EVERYTHING ELSE TO ME, OKAY?
THWIP-IP!
DEE-DEE-DEE
NEW ADDITION TO MY WEB-SHOOTERS: WEB-FLUID METER. THEY'RE ALMOST EMPTY.
I WAS SO WORRIED ABOUT AUNT MAY FALLING OUT...
...I USED UP ALL MY WEBS SEALING A HOLE THAT I MADE!
SO MUCH FOR WEB-CHUTES OR A WEB-CUSHION TO SOFTEN OUR LANDING.
HUZZAH.

SLINGSHOT ME!
THAT'S JAY'S PRIVATE JET!
MY AUNT MAY AND HER HUSBAND ARE ON BOARD!
PETER! I--I'LL HAVE TO HELP THE OTHERS.
THERE ARE JUMBO JETS GOING DOWN. THOUSANDS OF PEOPLE!
CAN YOU--?
GO!
I CAN DO THIS!
I HAVE TO.
RUNCHH

AVENGERS! NEW PROBLEM! PICKING UP AIR TRAFFIC CONTROL.
THAT BLAST TERMINUS DEFLECTED--
--JUST SHUT DOWN EVERY COMMERCIAL AIRCRAFT IN A TEN-MILE RADIUS!
I'LL KEEP AN EYE ON THE BOY! EVERYONE ELSE, GRAB A PLANE!
THW
EVERY COMMERCIAL--? OH NO!
CAPTAIN MARVEL!
CATC
GOT YOU, SPIDEY.
THOUGH I DON'T KNOW WHAT IT IS YOU THINK YOU CAN DO UP HERE.
JUST GO! I'LL KNOW WHEN I SEE--
THERE!

GYAH!
K-KOOM
ONE SIDE, AVENGERS! LET ALPHA SHOW YOU HOW IT'S DONE!
MY GOD.
HE-- HE WAS JUST IN TOKYO...
HE DIDN'T RUN. HE FLEW. HE USED SUPER-SPEED AND FLIGHT.
ALPHA HAD ONE LIMITATION: HE COULD ONLY USE ONE OF HIS POWERS AT A TIME.
NOW IT LOOKS LIKE THAT'S GONE.
TEENAGE BOY. POWERS OF A GOD, BRAIN OF A SLACKER--
-KEEP AY FROM ME!
--AND HE'S PICKING ON TERMINUS LIKE A SCHOOLYARD BULLY.
TELL ME HOW THIS ENDS WELL.

ENOUGH CHATTER. YOU HAVE ACCESS TO ALPHA? CALL HIM IN.
CAP, I DON'T THINK THAT'S--
YOU BEEN TRAINING HIM?
YES, BUT--
HE'S ONE OF OUR BIGGEST GUNS. MAKE THE CALL. NOW.
ALL RIGHT. BUT FOR THE RECORD, I OFFICIALLY OBJECT.
ALPHA, PICK UP.
WHO IS THIS? AND HOW'D YOU GET THIS VERY PRIVATE--
Y'KNOW DARN WELL WHO THIS IS. IT'S SPIDER-MAN.
HEY, BOY WONDER.
STOP. KID, THIS IS IT. THE ONE YOU'VE BEEN WAITING FOR. THE AVENGERS.
YOU JUST GOT CALLED UP TO THE MAJORS.
AWESOME! WHERE ARE YOU GUYS?
MANHAT--
SAY NO MORE. I AM ON...
...MY...
...WAY!

NOT MUCH. JUST AN ALIEN THREAT ABOUT TO DESTROY THE PLANET.
PEOPLE OF EARTH, HEAR ME! YOUR WORLD'S MINERALS, MOLTEN CORE, AND LIFE-ESSENCE ARE HERBY CLAIMED...
...IN THE NAME OF TERMINUS!
IS THAT ALL?
OH BOY.
SOMETHING TELLS ME AUNT MAY'S GONNA HAVE TO WAIT.

THIS'S CRAZY. I'M NOT GETTING ANYTHING DONE...
...AND MEANWHILE MY LIFE IS SLIPPING AWAY OUT THERE.
I PROMISED AUNT MAY I'D SAY GOODBYE BEFORE SHE LEFT...
STILL TIME.
IF I DO THIS SPIDEY-STYLE!
SOUTH STREET SEAPORT TO LA GUARDIA?
I MAY SET A FEW WEB-SWINGING RECORDS--BUT, YEAH, I CAN PULL THIS OFF.
AND WHO KNOWS?
GETTING SOME FRESH AIR AND STEPPING OUT OF MY "BOX," MIGHT BE JUST WHAT THE--
SPIDER-MAN! THERE YOU ARE.
--IRON MAN ORDERED.
SO YOU FINALLY ANSWERED ONE OF OUR CALLS.
YEP. THAT'S ME. YOU SAY "AVENGERS," I SAY "ASSEMBLE."
GOOD. 'CAUSE W
NEED EVERYBOD
ON THIS ONE.
REALLY? WHAT'S UP?

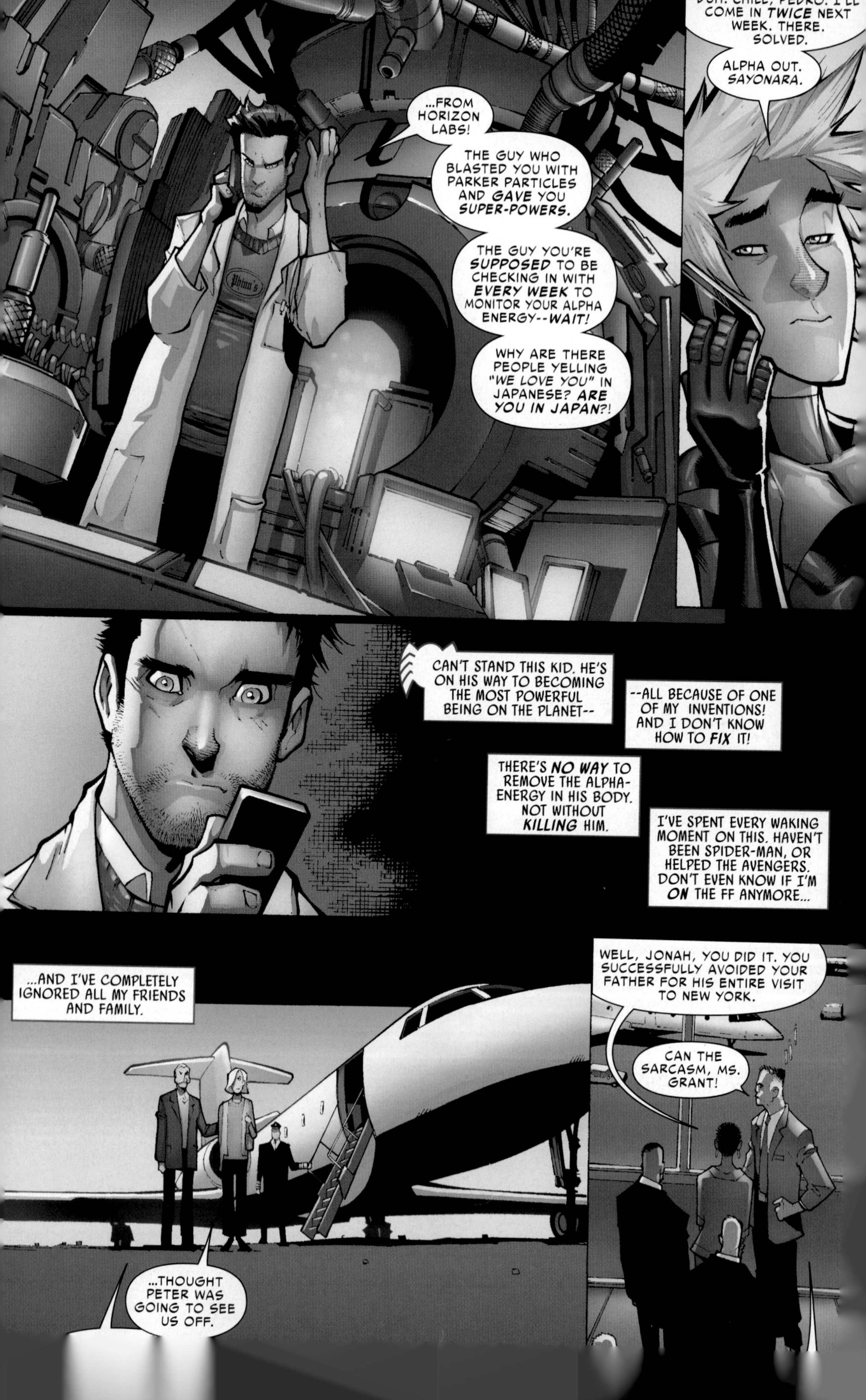
...FROM HORIZON LABS!
THE GUY WHO BLASTED YOU WITH PARKER PARTICLES AND GAVE YOU SUPER-POWERS.
THE GUY YOU'RE SUPPOSED TO BE CHECKING IN WITH EVERY WEEK TO MONITOR YOUR ALPHA ENERGY--WAIT!
WHY ARE THERE PEOPLE YELLING "WE LOVE YOU" IN JAPANESE? ARE YOU IN JAPAN?!
DUH. CHILL, PEDRO. I'LL COME IN TWICE NEXT WEEK. THERE. SOLVED.
ALPHA OUT. SAYONARA.
CAN'T STAND THIS KID. HE'S ON HIS WAY TO BECOMING THE MOST POWERFUL BEING ON THE PLANET--
--ALL BECAUSE OF ONE OF MY INVENTIONS! AND I DON'T KNOW HOW TO FIX IT!
THERE'S NO WAY TO REMOVE THE ALPHA-ENERGY IN HIS BODY. NOT WITHOUT KILLING HIM.
I'VE SPENT EVERY WAKING MOMENT ON THIS. HAVEN'T BEEN SPIDER-MAN, OR HELPED THE AVENGERS. DON'T EVEN KNOW IF I'M ON THE FF ANYMORE...
...AND I'VE COMPLETELY IGNORED ALL MY FRIENDS AND FAMILY.
...THOUGHT PETER WAS GOING TO SEE US OFF.
WELL, JONAH, YOU DID IT. YOU SUCCESSFULLY AVOIDED YOUR FATHER FOR HIS ENTIRE VISIT TO NEW YORK.
CAN THE SARCASM, MS. GRANT!

ALPHA
PART 3: FINAL GRADE
ALPHA
BRRING BRRING
THIS'S ALPHA. NOT HERE RIGHT NOW, PROBABLY OFF SAVING THE UNIVERSE OR SUMTHIN'.
IF YOU'RE ANYBODY FAMOUS, LET'S TALK WHEN I'M BACK FROM ALPHA-CON 2012.
IF YOU'RE A GIRL, LEAVE YOUR MEASUREMENTS. LATERS!
ANDREW? IT'S DAD. YOUR MOM AND I, WE--
--WE KNOW WE GOT CARRIED AWAY WITH ALL THIS. WE SCREWED UP. BUT HOW LONG ARE YOU GOING TO--?
LOOK, JUST COME HOME, SON. OR TALK TO US. CAN YOU DO THAT? PLEASE?
747
MARK, C'MON. I'M NOT SEEING HIM ANYMORE--
CAN'T STOP SEEING HIM. GUY'S EVERYWHERE.
IT WAS ONE TIME. I MEAN, HE'S A SUPER HERO. HOW WAS I SUPPOSE TO--?
UNH. ENOUGH WITH THE DRAMA ALL RIGHT? WE'R GONNA BE LATE FOR CLASS.
HELLO--
JOAN, WHERE ARE WE NOW?
TOKYO.
--TOKYO!
YOU ARE AWESOME! LOVE YA! THE ALPHA-DOG IS IN THE HOUSE!
BREEP BREEP
ONE SEC.
OKAY, WHO IS THIS AND HOW DID YOU GET THIS VERY PRIVATE NUMBER?
WHO DO YOU THINK? IT'S PETER, ANDREW.
PETER PARKER...

AMAZING SPIDER-MAN #694

Y JANE WATSON, GHT? THIS FOR L? WAIT--THIS A HOLOGRAM?
OR DID SOMEONE "WEIRD SCIENCE" YOU IN ONE OF THE LABS?
NO. I'M REALLY HERE. JUST VISITING A FRIEND.
YOU GUYS KNOW WHERE I CAN FIND PETER PARKER?
LAB SEVEN.
LUCKY SUNNUVA...
E ROOMS
LABS
HORIZON
MJ
, MR. P? YOU OKAY? VEN'T SEEN YOU IN A COUPLE DAYS.
BROUGHT YOU SOME TAPAS FROM THE CLUB.
RRY, MJ. BEEN SY. WITH WORK UFF. AVENGERS TUFF. SPIDEY STUFF.
AND TRAINING ALPHA.
SO YOU HAVEN'T GIVEN UP ON MINI-YOU YET? THAT'S GOOD, RIGHT?
NO. IT'S NOT. I'M PLAYING HIM.
TOLD HIM IF HE KEPT UP WITH THE SIDEKICKING--
--AND SHOWED UP HERE FOR REGULAR TESTS...
...THERE'S GOING TO BE A SPOT FOR YOU ON THE AVENGERS.
FOR REAL?
YOU'RE SAYING THERE'S NOT.
YEP.
AND THESE TESTS?
I HAVEN'T CRACKED IT YET, BUT I WILL. I HAVE TO TURN HIM BACK TO NORMAL.
HE'S JUST NOT... WORTHY.
YOU HAVE A SAY IN THAT?
DAMN STRAIGHT. HIS POWER IS MY RESPONSIBILITY. THAT GIVES ME ALL THE SAY I NEED.
AND I SAY...
ALPHA-- NO MORE.

I SAY AT ALL TI--
TO YOU.
JOAN, IT LOOKS LIKE I'M THE MOST SPECIAL THING IN THE WHOLE WORLD.
I SHOULD BE SETTING MY SIGHTS WAY HIGHER. CAN YOU MAKE IT HAPPEN?
FOR FIFTEEN PERCENT.
OF COURSE.
"THE YOUNG, SUPER-STAR, BAD-BOY HAS EMANCIPATED HIMSELF FROM HIS PARENTS...
"...MOVED INTO HIS OWN MANHATTAN PENTHOUSE, AND IS NOW IN CONTROL OF HIS OWN FORTUNE."
THIS WE
Sta
ALPHA FLYING SOLO!
UNDE COVER INSIDE
CAN YOU BELIEVE THIS KID?
ASK ME, WHAT HE NEEDS IS A GOOD BENJAMIN GRIMM TRADEMARKED CLOBBERIN'!
I SAY THE BALL IS STILL IN SPIDER-MAN' COURT. HE CAN DO THIS.
HE JUST NEEDS TO TAKE CHARGE AND PUT THE BOY ON THE RIGHT PATH.
WE'RE DOOMED
HERE, MAX. THERE'S A MORALITY CLAUSE IN MAGUIRE'S CONTRACT.
HE STEPS OUT NE, HORIZON CAN TANCE ITSELF FROM HIM.
. LEGALLY. EVERYTHING S HAPPENING ANDREW...
...WE BROUGHT THIS ON HIM. WE'RE TO BLAME. I JUST HOPE HE CAN FORGIVE US.
Y'KNOW I GOT ALL YOUR CALENDARS--
--AND A BIG POSTER O' YOU ON MY WALL?
MMM-- AWESOME!
MM-HMM--ME TOO.
GOT A POSTER OF YOU ON MY WALL.
"HEY, YOU'RE THAT SUPERMODEL AREN'T YA?..."

AND SPIDER-MAN? BE SURE TO LET YOUR BOY WONDER KNOW...
...THIS IS GOING ON HIS PERMANENT RECORD.
CLICK
ICK! NO. SORRY. THAT IS *STILL* WRONG.
JACKAL. "*PRINCESS.*" ALL OF 'EM. THAT'S IT?
SO WE WON?
YEAH. WE "*WON.*"
AND I MUST *NEVER* TELL KAINE ABOUT THIS. EVER.
EASY. HAVE YOU ALL FREE IN A SECOND.
SO THAT'S THE CHEERLEADER. THE PARENTS. AND YOU'RE...?
CONWAY.
JOAN CONWAY. HIS LAWYER. AND AGENT.
ANDY, THAT WAS INCREDIBLE. YOU SAVED US.
I DON'T KNOW HOW I COULD EVER--
LATER.
SON, WE'RE SORRY.
WE SHOU STOP. IT TOO RIS AND IT' NOT WOR IT. NOT IF MEANS
SAVE IT.
THINK I UNDERSTAND NOW. I W GETTING CAUGHT UP IN ALL TH LITTLE THINGS MY POWERS COULD GET ME.
BUT I KN I'VE ST GOT A L TO LEAR IF YOU' WILLING TEACH
ALL RIGHT, K *ONE* MORE SH BUT REMEMBE THERE ARE *RU*

IT'S THE ONE THING--
--THE ONLY THING THAT MAKES ME SPECIAL.
NO ONE'S TAKING IT FROM ME. I'D RATHER DIE.
NO. THAT'S NOT WHAT I WAS TRYING TO--
WITHOUT IT I'M A NOBODY!
NO BETTER THAN THESE STUPID, WORTHLESS THINGS!
SPLURKTCH
DEAR GOD...
OH GROW UP, YOU BIG BABY. THEY'RE JUST BIG GLOBS OF CLONE GOO.
SIGH. WASTE OF A PERFECTLY GOOD MORNING.
GUESS IT'S "BIG RED BUTTON TIME."

...FROM THE HOST ORGANISM!
VZHOOM
ARGHH!
OH NO! I KNOW HOW ALPHA'S POWER WORKS. IT'S MY SCIENCE THAT CREATED IT!
I'VE LOOKED INTO REMOVING IT FROM ANDY--AND IT CAN'T BE DONE!
NOT WITHOUT KILLING HIM!
ALPHA!
ANDY, YOU GOTTA HELP ME, KID! I CAN'T DO THIS ALONE!
I KNOW WHAT YOU'RE GOING THROUGH. YOU'RE HURTING, TIRED, AND IT'D BE SO EASY TO GIVE UP. BUT YOU CAN'T!
TRUST ME! WHEN YOU'RE TRAPPED UNDER SOME BIG, HEAVY THING--
--THAT'S WHEN YOU DIG DEEP!
YOUR FRIENDS AND FAMILY ARE HERE AND THEY NEED YOU! DO IT FOR THEM!
C'MON, HERO UP! WHOLE WORLD'S COUNTING ON YOU!
IF THE JACKAL GETS AHOLD OF THAT ALPHA-ENERGY--IF HE PULLS IT OUT OF YOU--
NO!
CAN'T--LET--THAT--HAPPEN--
GRAHH!

?
?
?
?
?
?
WHAT? WHY'RE YOU JUST STANDING THERE!
MAKE WITH THE JAZZ HANDS! DO THE ZAPPY-THING!
OH.
SHOOT.
THE ALPHA-ENERGY DIDN'T ALTER THE BRAT'S DNA. IT CAN'T BE CLONED, I GUESS.
AH, WELL... ON TO PLAN B.
HATE IT WHENEVER THEY SAY "PLAN B."
THAT'S SUPER VILLAIN CODE FOR "BLOW EVERYTHING UP."
ANDY! HANG ON!
I'M GETTING YOU OUT OF THAT THING!
HURRY...
TZEEE
OH NO YOU ON'T. THAT IS NOT ON THE SYLLABUS.
HSS
PRINCESS, QUEEN-CLONES, DO US A FAVOR...
...EAT THE HOSTAGES.
IN IT! CAN'T LET THAT HAPPEN.
REN KNOWS ME Y TOO WELL-- JUST HOW TO PLAY ME.
AND THIS IS WHY I NEED TO GET NEW VILLAINS...
FINE. IF THE ALPHA-ENERGY CAN'T BE DUPLICATED...
...I'LL JUST HAVE TO HARVEST IT...

EYEWWW!
HOLY MOTHER OF--
UGH!
WHAT IS--? AND IT SMELLS!
IS THAT PART OF A PANCREAS?
CLONE.
PLEASE, WHEN IT COMES TO ADVANCED SLUGFEST 101, I ALWAYS SEND IN A SUBSTITUTE.
IT'S A PRETTY SAFE BET THIS ISN'T EVEN ME RIGHT NOW.
BUT YOU KNOW WHAT IS REAL?
MY FIRST BATCH OF ALPHAS.
BEHOLD! A NEW RACE OF KINGS TO GO WITH MY GENETICALLY ENHANCED SPIDER QUEENS.
AN UNSTOPPABLE ARMY OF THE MOST POWERFUL BEINGS ON THE PLANET AND...
PTSSSSS
TZEE
NO...
...MINE TO CONTROL!
SO NOT GOOD.
THIS IS LIKE CLONING MOLECULE MAN, DARK PHOENIX, OR THE BEYONDER!
ONE ALPHA WAS BAD ENOUGH, BUT THIS? IT'S END OF THE WORLD TIME!
GNHH! YOU CAN'T DO THIS!
WON'T LET YOU--! AHH!
TZEE
AND HERE ENDETH THE LESSON.
GOODBYE, SPIDER-MAN.
ALPHA-MALES...
DESTROY HIM!

WHEN YOU CREATED ALPHA, YOU "OUT-MAD-SCIENCED" ME.
THIS FAILURE OF YOURS HAS TOPPED ALL OF MY SUCCESSES.
AH! THE STUDENT HAS BECOME THE MASTER.
EXCEPT FOR THE PART WHERE MY SPIDERZONS TOOK YOU OUT ON THE PLAYGROUND AND SCHOOLED YA.
WHAT'S UP WITH THAT?
WAIT. THEIR STINGERS ARE BASED ON SPIDER-BIOLOGY. THEY SHOULDN'T HAVE WORKED ON YOU AT ALL...
PSST. HEY, TEACH. GUESS WHAT?
ACTING!

WHO ARE YOU? WHY ARE YOU DOING THIS?!
WHAT DO YOU WANT FROM ME?
SO MANY QUESTIONS, MR. MAGUIRE. NEXT TIME RAISE YOUR HAND.
SORRY. MY BAD. FORGOT ABOUT THE CARBONADIUM SHACKLES AND THE WHITE SOUND HELMET.
ACTUALLY, IT'S IMPRESSIVE YOU CAN EVEN TALK.
WELL, DEAR BOY, I AM DR. MILES WARREN, ALSO KNOWN AS THE JACKAL.
AND I'M HERE TO MAKE YOUR DREAM COME TRUE. I'M GONNA PUT YOUR FACE EVERYWHERE.
YOU SEE, I'M GOING TO USE YOU-- OR RATHER YOUR CLONES--TO POPULATE THE EARTH--
--MY EARTH. A PERFECT WORLD OF ALPHA-MALES.
HAHAHAHA
TZEE TZEE TZEEE
AND WHAT DO WE HAVE HERE?
WHY IT'S ONE OF MY OLD STUDENTS. LATE TO CLASS AGAIN.
YOU'LL HAVE TO GET NOTES FROM SOMEONE ELSE. I'M NOT STARTING OVER.
J-JACKAL. WHAT DO YOU--
OH HOW CAN I STAY MAD AT MY STAR PUPIL?
ESPECIALLY WHEN YOU MADE AL OF THIS POSSIBLE MR. PARKER.

WHOEVER DID THIS COULD TAKE OUT ALPHA. THAT'S PRETTY HARDCORE.
MAYBE I SHOULD CALL IN SOME AVENGER-Y BACKUP?
HM. NO RECEPTION.
MUST BE IN A DEAD ZONE OR--
HSSSAH!
AAAND SPEAKING OF RECEPTION.
LADIES? YOU DO KNOW I HAVE SPIDER-SENSE, RIGHT?
KLIKK KIKK IK!
THOK
WAP
FWAK
B-DEEP B-DEEP
AND SPIDER-FU! CAN'T OVERLOOK THE FU!
WORKS GREAT AGAINST ALL SPIDER-BASED BAD-GUYS...
AND ANY SPIDERY-ATTACK...
HAKK
...THEY CAN DISH...
TEK
KLIK IKK IKK!
...OUT.
"WHAT ARE THOSE THINGS...?"

LET'S HOPE THIS WORKS.
WE TOOK ORGANIC FIBERS FROM CLOTHES ANDY WAS WEARING WHEN HE WAS FIRST HIT BY ALPHA-ENERGY...
...AND SPLICED 'EM INTO MY "FRIEND" SPIDER-MAN'S SPIDER-TRACER TECHNOLOGY.
THE SIMILAR CHARGE SHOULD LEAD ME RIGHT TO HIM.
B-DEEP B-DEEP
BINGO!
DO NOT
NEVER COULD'VE PIECED THIS TOGETHER WITHOUT MAX'S HELP.
I'M LUCKY...
...LUCKY TO HAVE PEOPLE LIKE MAX MODELL IN MY LIFE
AND ROLE MODELS LIKE CAPTAIN STACY, UNCLE BEN, AND AUNT MAY.
END OF THE DAY, IT'S NOT ANY RADIOACTIVE SPIDER BITE THAT'S MADE ME SPIDER-MAN...
B-DEEP B-DEEP
...IT'S TRYING TO LIVE UP TO THEIR EXAMPLES--TO BE A PERSON THEY'D BE PROUD OF.
MJ'S RIGHT. THAT'S WHAT'S MISSING WITH ALPHA. AND MAYBE...
...IF WE GET THROUGH THIS, AND I PLAY MY PART RIGHT, I CAN BE THAT KIND OF PERSON FOR HIM.
HMM. ABANDONED SCHOOL IN BROOKLYN.
B-DEEP B-DEEP
OY. WHY CAN'T BAD GUYS EVER HAVE A SECRET LAIR THAT DOESN'T REQUIRE A TETANUS SHOT?

THIS IS VERY TRICKY.
ONE OF THE UNIQUE PROPERTIES OF ALPHA-ENERGY IS THAT IT *DOESN'T* LEAVE A RESIDUAL TRAIL.
IT'S SO WONDERFULLY CLEAN AND ENVIRONMENTALLY SAFE. I HAD SUCH HIGH HOPES FOR IT.
SORRY. UM, MR. MODELL?
I'VE GIVEN IT A LOT OF THOUGHT. AND ONCE WE'VE FOUND ANDY AND THE OTHERS...
...I SHOULD PROBABLY LEAVE HORIZON LABS.
WHY?
ALL THE TROUBLE YOU'VE HAD RECENTLY-- IT'S BEEN 'CAUSE OF *ME* OR MY RELATIONSHIP WITH SPIDER-MAN.
ALPHA. THE DISRUPTION OF MORBIUS' DRUG TRIALS. WHEN I DIDN'T DOUBLE-CHECK GRADY'S TIME DOOR.
YOU'D *ALL* BE BETTER OFF WITHOUT ME.
PETER, YOU'VE GIVEN HORIZON SOME OF ITS *BEST* INVENTIONS.
AND AS FAR AS YOUR *"RELATIONSHIP"* WITH SPIDER-MAN GOES...
..BECAUSE OF IT *WE* OPPED A VIRUS FROM FECTING THE CITY. *WE* OCATED DOC OCK'S CRET BASE BEFORE HE ULD DESTROY THE WORLD.
THANKS TO THE TWO OF YOU, WE'RE NO LONGER *JUST* A PLACE THAT MAKES TECH.
WE GET TO BE *HEROES.*
I WOULDN'T TRADE THAT FOR ANYTHING. NOW, IF YOU DON'T MIND, I'D LIKE TO FINISH THIS BUILD...
...AND HELP SPIDER-MAN SAVE THE DAY. *AGAIN.* YOU WITH ME?
YOU GOT IT, COACH!

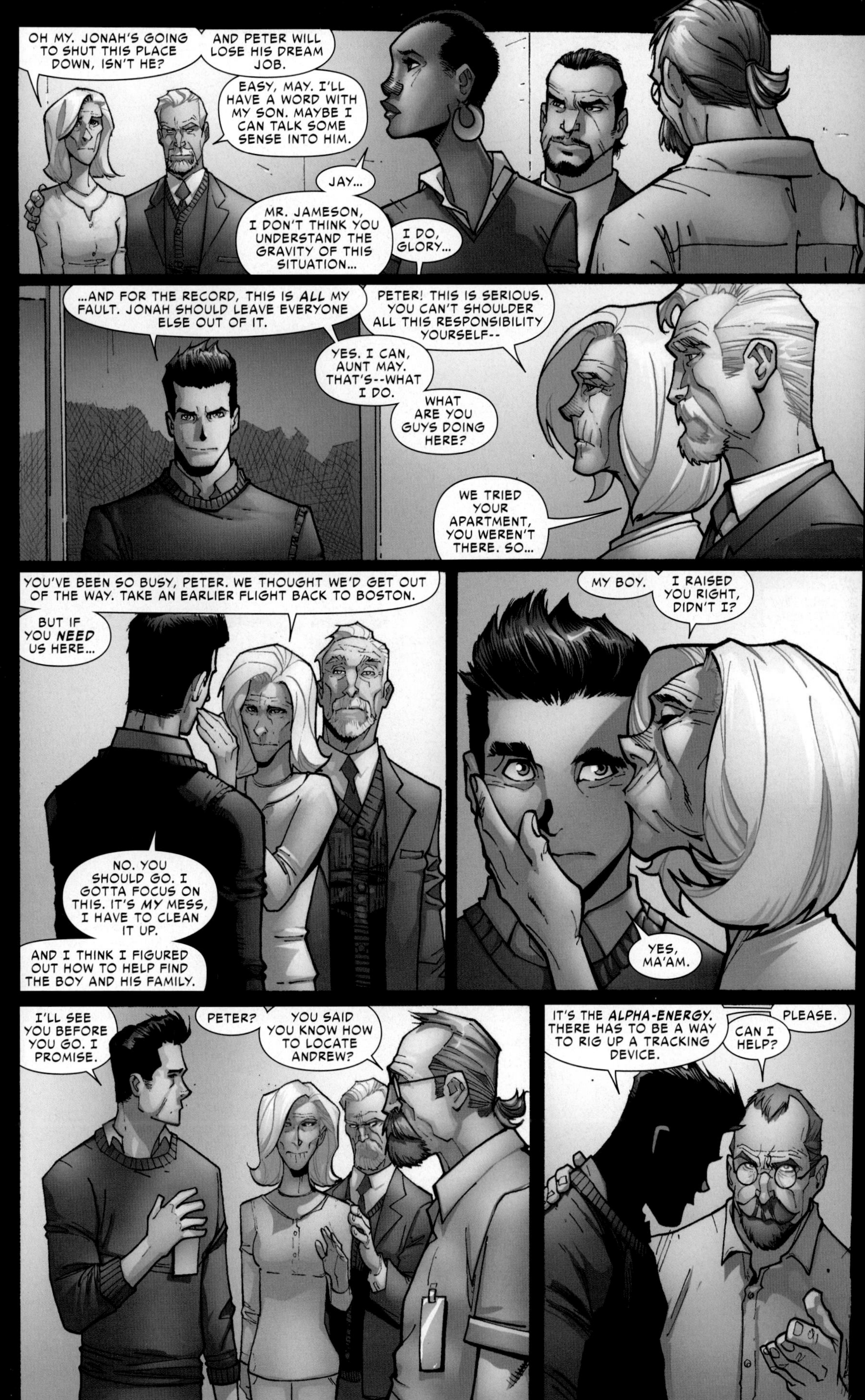
OH MY. JONAH'S GOING TO SHUT THIS PLACE DOWN, ISN'T HE?
AND PETER WILL LOSE HIS DREAM JOB.
EASY, MAY. I'LL HAVE A WORD WITH MY SON. MAYBE I CAN TALK SOME SENSE INTO HIM.
JAY...
MR. JAMESON, I DON'T THINK YOU UNDERSTAND THE GRAVITY OF THIS SITUATION...
I DO, GLORY...
...AND FOR THE RECORD, THIS IS ALL MY FAULT. JONAH SHOULD LEAVE EVERYONE ELSE OUT OF IT.
PETER! THIS IS SERIOUS. YOU CAN'T SHOULDER ALL THIS RESPONSIBILITY YOURSELF--
YES. I CAN, AUNT MAY. THAT'S--WHAT I DO.
WHAT ARE YOU GUYS DOING HERE?
WE TRIED YOUR APARTMENT, YOU WEREN'T THERE. SO...
YOU'VE BEEN SO BUSY, PETER. WE THOUGHT WE'D GET OUT OF THE WAY. TAKE AN EARLIER FLIGHT BACK TO BOSTON.
BUT IF YOU NEED US HERE...
NO. YOU SHOULD GO. I GOTTA FOCUS ON THIS. IT'S MY MESS, I HAVE TO CLEAN IT UP.
AND I THINK I FIGURED OUT HOW TO HELP FIND THE BOY AND HIS FAMILY.
MY BOY.
I RAISED YOU RIGHT, DIDN'T I?
YES, MA'AM.
I'LL SEE YOU BEFORE YOU GO. I PROMISE.
PETER?
YOU SAID YOU KNOW HOW TO LOCATE ANDREW?
IT'S THE ALPHA-ENERGY. THERE HAS TO BE A WAY TO RIG UP A TRACKING DEVICE.
CAN I HELP?
PLEASE.

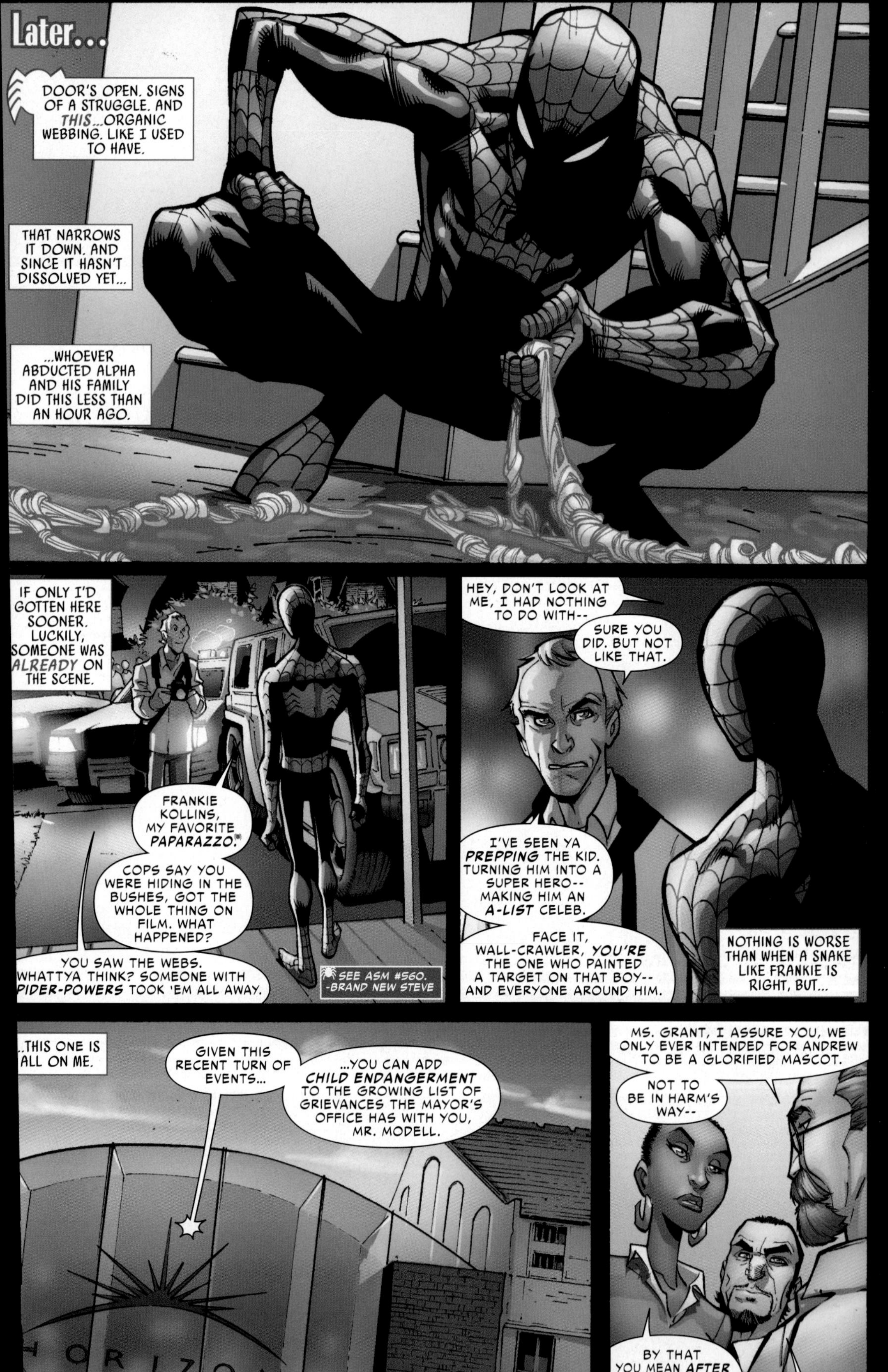

Later...
DOOR'S OPEN. SIGNS OF A STRUGGLE. AND THIS...ORGANIC WEBBING. LIKE I USED TO HAVE.
THAT NARROWS IT DOWN. AND SINCE IT HASN'T DISSOLVED YET...
...WHOEVER ABDUCTED ALPHA AND HIS FAMILY DID THIS LESS THAN AN HOUR AGO.
IF ONLY I'D GOTTEN HERE SOONER. LUCKILY, SOMEONE WAS ALREADY ON THE SCENE.
FRANKIE KOLLINS, MY FAVORITE PAPARAZZO.*
COPS SAY YOU WERE HIDING IN THE BUSHES, GOT THE WHOLE THING ON FILM. WHAT HAPPENED?
YOU SAW THE WEBS. WHATTYA THINK? SOMEONE WITH SPIDER-POWERS TOOK 'EM ALL AWAY.
*SEE ASM #560. -BRAND NEW STEVE
HEY, DON'T LOOK AT ME, I HAD NOTHING TO DO WITH--
SURE YOU DID. BUT NOT LIKE THAT.
I'VE SEEN YA PREPPING THE KID. TURNING HIM INTO A SUPER HERO-- MAKING HIM AN A-LIST CELEB.
FACE IT, WALL-CRAWLER, YOU'RE THE ONE WHO PAINTED A TARGET ON THAT BOY-- AND EVERYONE AROUND HIM.
NOTHING IS WORSE THAN WHEN A SNAKE LIKE FRANKIE IS RIGHT, BUT...
...THIS ONE IS ALL ON ME.
GIVEN THIS RECENT TURN OF EVENTS...
...YOU CAN ADD CHILD ENDANGERMENT TO THE GROWING LIST OF GRIEVANCES THE MAYOR'S OFFICE HAS WITH YOU, MR. MODELL.
HORIZON
MS. GRANT, I ASSURE YOU, WE ONLY EVER INTENDED FOR ANDREW TO BE A GLORIFIED MASCOT.
NOT TO BE IN HARM'S WAY--
BY THAT YOU MEAN AFTER THE INDUSTRIAL ACCIDENT WHICH COULD HAVE KILLED HIM?
MAX, DON'T ANSWER THAT.

THAT'S IT! WHATEVER YOU ARE, YOU ARE SO IN FOR IT! YOU'RE FACING ALPHA NOW!
AH!
ZRAK
STAY BACK. OR DO SOMETHING USEFUL.
LIKE WHAT?
I DUNNO. A CHEER? THAT'D ACTUALLY BE KINDA COOL.
OH, ALPHA!
SO STRONG, SO BRAVE...
...SO STUPID!
HAKK AKK AKK
UNH!
TEK
TIK
I SWEAR, IT'S LIKE THE BOY DOESN'T KNOW HIS OWN POWERS.
HE CAN ONLY USE ONE AT A TIME. GO WITH THE ZAPPY-HANDS, THAT MEANS NO FORCE FIELD.
ROOKIE MISTAKE.
AGREED. IF YOU ASK ME...
...I BLAME HIS TEACHER.
CLEARLY, SOMEONE WASN'T DOING THEIR JOB.

ISSY, WAIT! HIS ISN'T WHAT--
OKAY, THIS IS EXACTLY HAT IT LOOKS LIKE.
BUT I CAN EXPLAIN--
YOU CAN EXPLAIN PAULA LAKE?!
SHE CAME OVER. AND WELL...
C'MON. SHE'S A *CHEERLEADER.*
GO TO *HELL!*
...AAAAND THERE GOES THE WEB-PAGE.
WAIT. HE HAS *ANOTHER* GIRL UP THERE?
EXCUSE ME. ES *ANDREW GUIRE* LIVE HERE?
DYING TO MEET HIM.
DR. WARREN. D MY GIRL, *RINCESS,* RE IS A BIG ALPHA FAN.
UGE.
THIS IS GETTING RIDICULOUS. IT'S LIKE A REVOLVING DOOR IN HERE.
JOAN, WHEN YO MOVE US INTO THE CITY WE'RE GOING TO NEED SECURITY.
AGREED. AND HAVE A TALK WITH YOUR SON.
OR YOU'RE GONNA HAVE A LOT OF BIEBER-STYLE PATERNITY SUIT ON YOUR HANDS
HSSSS
NOW YOU'VE DONE IT.
YOU UPSE PRINCESS
AHHH
WHAT'S GOING ON DOWN--
MOM! DAD!

THE WHOLE WORLD. EVERYONE KNOWS WHO ANDY IS!
AND NOW HE'S NOT JUST SOME CELEBRITY--SOME KID ON A COMMERCIAL. HE'S THE REAL THING.
CAN'T BELIEVE THIS'S HAPPENING!
I'M DATING A SUPER HERO!
NO. I AM DATING THE SUPER HERO.
BETTER THAN ALL THE FF COMBINED.
AND SPIDER-MAN--IS--HIS--SIDEKICK!
OKAY. CALM DOWN. DEEP BREATH.
AHH!
I'M LOIS LANE!
FATHER? I'M CONFUSED. I THOUGHT LOIS LANE WAS "POP CULTURE." A FICTIONAL CHARACTER.
SHE IS. THE GIRL WAS DRAWING AN ANALOGY, PRINCESS.
AH. SHOULD WE KILL HER?
NO. WAIT.
NOK NOK
HI, MR. MAGUIRE. IS ALPHA HOME? IT'S CHRISSY.
CHRISSY?
LET HER IN.
IT'S THE GIRL WHO RUNS ALPHA'S WEBSITE.
JOAN, DID YOU HIRE HER?
IT'S A FAN SITE. GETS A LOT OF TRAFFIC. IT'S GOOD FOR US.
BUT IS IT MONETIZED? 'CAUSE IF IT IS--
RAY. ALICE. I'M ON TOP OF THIS.
IT'S OKAY. I KNOW THE WAY.
OHMIGOD! ANDY, YOU WERE AMAZING LAST NIGHT!
YOU HAVE TO TELL ME ALL ABOUT IT!
WHAT'S THE HUMAN TORCH REALLY--
--LIKE?

OKAY, TIGER...
...TELL ME YOUR TROUBLES.
SPILL.
WHAT YOU SAID EARLIER. ABOUT ALPHA. YOU WERE RIGHT.
I LOOK AT HIM, AND I DON'T SEE A YOUNG JOHNNY STORM.
OR SOME SUPER-POWERED, BOY-VERSION OF LINDSAY LOHAN.
I SEE *ME*. AND EVERYTHING I *WOULD* HAVE BECOME IF NOT FOR--
YOU KNOW.
IF YOUR UNCLE BEN HADN'T DIED?
YEAH.
PETER PARKER, YOU'RE NOT WHO YOU ARE BECAUSE YOUR UNCLE BEN *DIED*.
YOU'RE WHO YOU ARE BECAUSE YOUR UNCLE BEN *LIVED*.
ALL THE GIFTS HE GAVE YOU, EVERYTHING YOU NEEDED, WAS ALREADY IN THERE.
D *LIKE* TO LIEVE THAT, J. I WOULD.
BUT ON, HAVE EVER MET ONE MORE -CENTERED HAN *ME*?
INSIDE I KNOW. IF IT WASN'T FOR THAT *ONE* NIGHT. THAT TRAGEDY...
...I WOULDN'T'VE SPENT THE REST OF MY LIFE WORRYING ABOUT LOSING EVERYBODY ELSE. HIDING BEHIND A MASK SO I COULD PROTECT--
CAN'T BELIEVE IT. I DID IT AGAIN.
I GOTTA GO.
SUDDENLY? JUST LIKE OLD TIMES.
GOT SO WRAPPED UP IN THE ME-ME-ME OF IT ALL, I DIDN'T STOP TO THINK...
ALPHA DOESN'T HAVE A MASK.

VRRHZZ
HERE.
WHAT? BUT SUBTERRANEA...
YOU MIGHT RUN INTO THE MOLE MAN AND MOLOIDS AND OTHER MOLE-RELATED THINGIES.
I COULD LEND A HAND. SHOOT SOME WEBS. AND DON'T FORGET ABOUT MY ALWAYS USEFUL SPIDER-SENSE. PERFECT FOR ANY--
NO. YOU HAVE MORE IMPORTANT THINGS TO DO.
THAT BOY TOOK OUT GIGANTO. WITH ONE PUNCH. AND HIS POWER'S GROWING.
HE IS THE ONLY ALPHA-LEVEL THREAT IN EXISTENCE--
BUT--
--AND HE'S YOUR RESPONSIBILITY.
SO THAT'S IT THEN? FROM NOW ON I'M JUST SOME KINDA GLORIFIED BABYSITTER?
NONSENSE. BABY-SITTERS GET PAID.
PERFECT.
TIMES LIKE THIS, I NEED A SHOULDER TO CRY ON.
AND THERE'S ONLY ONE PERSON I KNOW WHO GETS EVERYTHING I'M GOING THROUGH--
--IN AND OUT OF MY SPANDEX. HOPE SHE'S IN.
HEY, PETE. WELCOME BACK TO MJ'S. WHAT CAN I GET YA?
HI, KIM. CAN YOU POUR ME A--
NOTHING FOR MR. PARKER. HE'S ON CALL.
MOVE OVER. I'VE GOT THIS.
WAIT. YOU SAID HE WAS A SCIENTIST. HOW CAN HE BE "ON CALL?"
TRUST ME. PETER PARKER IS ALWAYS ON CALL.
I WAS GONNA SAY "CUP A' COFFEE." SHEESH.

EASY, SUE, ALMOST THERE. GOOD. DRILL CAR ONE IS SECURE.
BEN, BRING DRILL CAR TWO AROUND TO GIGANTO'S RIGHT SHOULDER...
LOOKS LIKE ALPHA'S WORK HERE IS DONE. I'LL LEAVE THE CLEANING UP TO THE PROFESSIONALS.
KID, TWO THINGS.
ONE, NEVER TALK ABOUT YOURSELF IN THE THIRD PERSON...
...SAYS "YOUR FRIENDLY NEIGHBORHOOD SPIDER-MAN."
...REPORTING LIVE FROM YANCY STREET, WHERE TEEN SENSATION ALPHA SINGLE-HANDEDLY DEFEATED ONE OF THE FANTASTIC FOUR'S MOST FEARSOME FOES.
ALPHA'S SIDEKICK, SPIDER-MA WAS ON HAN TO ADD A B OF COLOR A PROVIDE MOR SUPPORT.
50 NEWS
50 NEWS
ALPHA
PART 2: THAT SOMETHING SPECIAL
AND TWO, THIS IS A TEAM EFFORT. YOU CAN'T JUST TAKE OFF WHENEVER YOU FEEL--
SORRY, DIDN'T CATCH THAT. ANYHOO...
SCHOOL NIGHT. GOTTA GO.
PLACES TO SEE. PEOPLE TO DO.
ZZOW
SO THIS KID U'RE SIDEKICKING FOR--
HE'S THE SIDEKICK.
BRASH. IMPULSIVE. KINDA LIKE ME AT THAT AGE, RIGHT?
ELL, NOW OFFICIAL,
WHAT?
I HATE
ALL RIGHT, STRETCHO, WE'RE GOOD TO GO.
EXCELLENT WORK, BEN. YOU AND JOHNNY TAKE CAR TWO.
SUE AND I WILL BE IN CAR ONE. WE SHOULD REACH SUBTERRANEA IN UNDER THREE HOURS.
HEY, REED, WHAT ABOUT YOURS TRULY? WHERE DO YOU WANT ME?

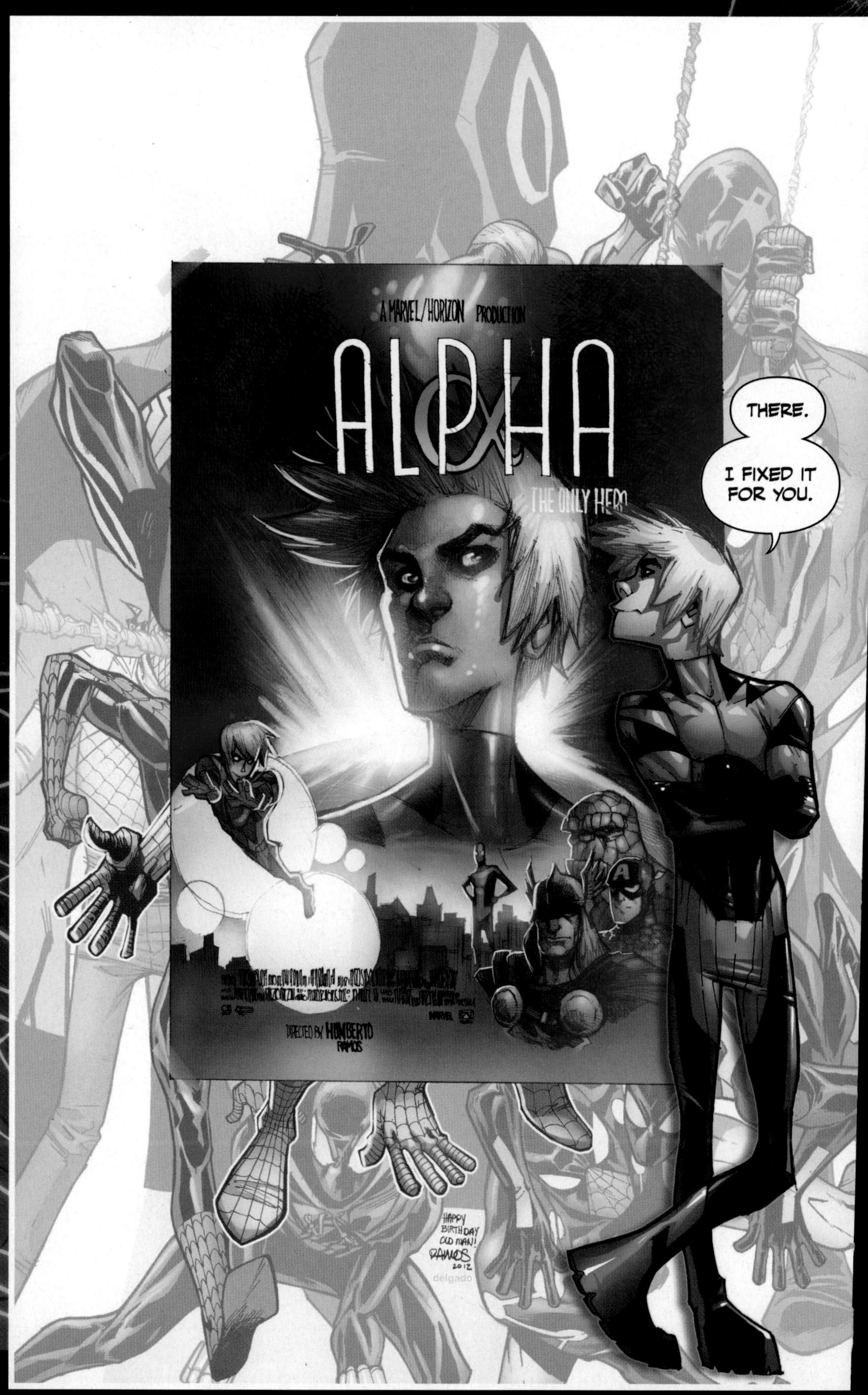

AMAZING SPIDER-MAN #693
COVER BY HUMBERTO RAMOS & EDGAR DELGADO

THERE ARE RULES! YA DON'T HEAR ME SAYIN' "THING SMASH!" OR "FLAME ON!" DO YA?!
I GOT RIGHTS!
YOU TOLD HIM? THE FIRST ALPHA-LEVEL THREAT IN EXISTENCE...
...AND YOU THOUGHT THE BEST COURSE OF ACTION WAS TO TELL HIM?
DO YOU REALIZE WHAT YOU'VE DONE?
YEAH.
IN EVERY POSSIBLE WAY...
...I'VE CREATED A MONSTER.
Elsewhere...
SO...GREAT POWER. GREAT RESPONSIBILITY. A TEEN OUTCAST.
AND A SCIENCE EXPERIMENT GONE AWRY. HISTORY REPEATS ITSELF.
HISTORY. NEVER WAS MY BEST SUBJECT. NOW BIOLOGY, CHEMISTRY, AND ALL-THINGS-PETER-PARKER?
BREAKING NEWS
OH, THE JACKAL CAN TEACH YOU A THING OR TWO ABOUT THOSE!
COME ALONG, GIRLS. PARKER PARTICLES? ALPHA-ENERGY?!
I GOTTA GET ME SOME A' THAT!
HAHAHAHAHAHAHAHAHAHAHAHAHAHAHA!
TIME
NEXT!
Spidey's 50th continues with the return of THE JACKAL!
(And if you know the Jackal at all...that can only mean one thing!)
BE HERE!

SEE A REAL HERO, PEOPLE?! HOW'S THAT?!
THE NAME'S ALPHA! THE MOST POWERFUL SUPER HERO OF 'EM ALL!
THAT'S RIGHT! AND MR. FANTASTIC AND THE AVENGERS, THEY'RE GETTING ME READY FOR THE BIG LEAGUES!
PUT ME IN THEIR "SIDEKICK PROGRAM" AND EVERYTHING. EVEN GAVE ME SPIDER-MAN AS A SIDEKICK! COOL, RIGHT?
AMAZING!
ONE PUNCH!
ALL THE FANTASTIC FOUR AROUND AND HE JUST--
ALPHA! OVER HERE!
THAT ROCKED!
WHY THAT COCKY LITTLE...
NICE GOING, WEBS.
"SIDEKICK"?
EASY, BEN!
UNBELIEVABL
I GOT THAT LINE TRADEMARKED, YA SNOT-NOSED LITTLE PUNK!

IT'S THAT ALPHA KID!
FROM THE COMMERCIALS?
YUP! EVERYBODY GET YOUR aPHONES READY...
...YOU'LL WANNA RECORD THIS!
THINK I DON'T KNOW WHAT YOU WERE DOING, SPIDEY? THIS WAS A TEST. AND FOR THE FIRST TIME EVER...
...ANDY MAGUIRE'S GETTIN' AN "A"!
SWITCHING FROM FLIGHT TO SUPER-STRENGTH. HERE IT COMES...
IIIIIT'S CLOBERRIN' TIME!
BA-KA-WHOOM
ALPHA!
HE--? DID HE JUST--? WITH THE--?
OHHHH NO, HE DIDN'T!

WRARK!
HOW'S MY FAVORITE FANTASTIC FOURSOME?
WHAT'S UP? IS MOLE MAN ATTACKING THE SURFACE WORLD AGAIN?
NOT THIS TIME, SPIDEY. IT'S JUST GIGANTO. REED? CAN YOU...?
I BELIEVE THE CREATURE'S IN ITS MATING SEASON. ACTING OUT UNTIL HE FINDS A MATE....
...BUT THE PROBLEM IS, HE MIGHT JUST BE THE LAST OF HIS KIND!
YANCY
WHOA! SO YOU'RE SAYING THIS IS A...GIANT MONSTER BOOTY CALL?
WITH NO BOOTY.
I SUGGESTED WE STUFF BEN IN A DRESS, BUT--
STILL NOT FUNNY, MATCHSTICK!
MY FORCE FIELDS AREN'T SLOWING HIM DOWN--

50% OFF
1962 PRICES!
TV
WHAT'D I SAY ABOUT REGULAR CROOKS?
THEY GET REGULAR PUNCHES.
BECAUSE?
YOU BREAK 'EM, YOU BUY 'EM.
AND?
HEALTHCARE AIN'T CHEAP.
BREEP BREEP
STOP. GETTING A CALL FROM THE FANTASTIC FOUR...
SWEET! WE'RE GONNA HAVE A TEAM-UP!
DON'T EVER CALL IT THAT. AND NO, WE'RE NOT.
AND WHEN FIGHTING SUPER VILLAINS?
THEY GET SUPER-PUNCHES?
NOW YOU'RE GETTIN' IT.
WHO'S MY LUDICROUSLY POWERED ZIT-MACHINE. YOU ARE. YES, YOU ARE.
THIS IS FOR SOMETHING BIG. WAY OUT OF YOUR LEAGUE.
BUT I THOUGHT I WAS THE END-ALL-BE-ALL, SUPER-POWER-WISE.
YOU'RE NOT READY FOR THIS. SO LET ME BE PERFECTLY CLEAR. STAY HERE. DO NOTHING. GOT IT?
SO...
ALL THIS POWER. ALL THIS RESPONSIBILITY. STAY HERE. DO NOTHING.
I SEE WHERE YOU'RE GOING WITH ALL OF THIS.

...WITH THAT POWER *MUST ALSO* COME THE *GREATEST* RESPONSIBILITY OF US ALL.
THAT'S HUGE. SO? YOU UP FOR IT?
I CAN TEACH YOU HOW TO DO THIS, BUT *ONLY* IF YOU FOLLOW MY RULES. BREAK 'EM, AND WE'RE DONE. UNDERSTOOD?
RULE NUMBER ONE?
SAVIN LIVES ALW COMES F
RULE NUMBER TWO?
SEE NUM O
YEAH. NO WORRIES.
WOW! ME, WORKING WITH AN AVENGER. THIS IS *SO* HAPPENING!

THAT'S IT. I'M OUTTA HERE.
WHERE ARE YOU GOING?
ON PATROL!
JUST WAIT, THEY'LL SEE...
...I'M GONNA SHOW 'EM WHAT A REAL HERO CAN DO!
WHOA! EASY THERE, BLONDIE. LET'S THROW SOME BRAKES ON THAT TRAIN.
SPIDER-MAN! AWESOME! WHAT'RE YOU DOING HERE?
ACTUALLY, KID? I WAS ON MY WAY TO SEE YOU.
REALLY?!
LLY. I HAD A TALK H MR. FANTASTIC THE REST OF THE ANDEX BRIGADE...
...AND WE DECIDED YOU NEED TO BE IN THE "SIDEKICK PROGRAM" AND THAT I WAS THE RIGHT GUY FOR THE JOB.
NO WAY! WHEN I'M NOT AROUND, YOU ALL TALK ABOUT ME?
YEAH. ALPHA, YOU HAVE GREAT POWER IN YOU. IN TIME, YOU MIGHT HAVE THE GREATEST POWER OF US ALL.
THAT MEANS NOW'S THE TIME YOU HAVE TO LEARN...

"...HE'S DOING EVERYTHING YOU WANTED TO DO...
"...BACK WHEN YOU WERE IN HIGH SCHOOL."
MMMMM
MMMMMM
HEY. I GOT SOMETHING SPECIAL I WANNA SHOW YOU.
OKAY.
YOU'RE GONNA LOV
THIS.
CHECK IT OUT! I DESIGNED MY OWN ALPHA FAN PAGE!
THAT'S... UH...REAL GREAT THERE, CHRISSY.
HEY! HAVE YOU READ THESE THREADS?
SORRY. HAVEN'T SET UP MODS FOR THE COMMENT SECTION YET.
HE'S A LOSER. POSER. SPAZ. DORK. LAME.
POOCHIE? WHAT'S A "POOCHIE"
A MASS TOOL AN NOT A R HERO?

PETER, WE NEED TO TALK.
SURE, JAY. WHAT'S UP?
WHAT DO YOU THINK THAT'S ABOUT?
BOY STUFF, OBVIOUSLY.
SHE WON'T COME OUT AND SAY IT, BUT YOUR AUNT'S WORRIED ABOUT YOU.
EVER SINCE WE MOVED TO BOSTON, IT'S LIKE YOU'VE *FORGOTTEN* WE EXIST.
THE WORLD ALMOST ENDED A FEW WEEKS AGO. YOU NEVER CALLED.
I WAS... BUSY.
EVERYONE'S BUSY. WHEN THINGS ARE IMPORTANT, YOU FIND THE TIME. UNDERSTOOD?
YES, SIR.
SEE ASM #686. -STEVE
AND DON'T FORGET TO DROP BY THE CLUB. I WANNA SHOW YOU OFF.
OF COURSE, DEAR.
SO? ARE THEY BACK TOGETHER?
I HAVE *NO* IDEA.
HE WILL, TOO. FOR MORE ON PETE'S TRIP WITH AUNT MAY, SEE AVENGING SPIDER-MAN #11. -SW
WHAT'S THE MATTER, TIGER? YOU WERE A MILLION MILES AWAY. THIS IS SOME SPIDEY-RELATED THING, ISN'T IT?
IS IT THAT KID FROM THE NEWS? THE ONE YOU ZAPPED WITH YOUR DOOHICKEY?
YEAH. I'VE BEEN KEEPING TABS ON HIM. AND...
...HE'S SUCH A *JERK*, MJ.
FLAUNTING HIS POWER. SHOWING OFF. PUSHING KIDS AROUND.
GOTCHA. SO BASICALLY YOU CAN'T STAND THIS KID BECAUSE...

PETER?
WHAT?
YOUR AUNT WAS TRYING TO TELL YOU SOMETHING.
SORRY, AUNT MAY. I WAS JUST THINKING ABOUT--
Y'SEE, THERE'S THIS THING WITH WORK AND--
NEVER MIND. WON'T HAPPEN AGAIN. YOU WERE SAYING?
JUST THAT JAY AND I WERE SORRY WE COULDN'T MAKE IT INTO TOWN LAST WEEK FOR YOUR BIG PRESENTATION.
ACTUALLY? I'M KINDA GLAD YOU WEREN'T THERE.
IT WAS A DISASTER.
OH MY. IS YOUR JOB OKAY?
I HOPE SO. YOU LOVE IT THERE. IT'S PRACTICALLY ALL YOU TALK ABOUT ANYMORE.
YEAH. IT'S FINE. BUT YOU'RE RIGHT, I DO GO ON ABOUT IT.
WHY DON'T WE CHANGE THE SUBJECT? YOU KNOW MJ'S GOT HER OWN NIGHTCLUB NOW.
REALLY?
YOU TWO WOULD LOVE IT. YOU HAVE TO COME OVER.
FAMILY. FRIENDS. SHOULD BE HAVI A GREAT TIME.
BUT ALL I CA THINK ABOUT THAT DUMB K

EASY. COMING IN FOR A LANDING.
ANDY! OVER HERE!
I LOVE ALPHA
YOU'RE CRAZY, CHRISSY. IF HE HADN'T PUSHED YOU OUTTA THE WAY, YOU'D BE A SUPER HERO NOW.
SHUT UP, MARK.
HEY, CHRISSY. NICE SHIRT.
IT'S THE ONLY ALPHA ONE THEY MAKE RIGHT NOW.
I'VE GOT SIX.
WE GOT SOME NEW ONES IN.
WHY DON'T YOU COME BY MY "SECRET LAIR" TONIGHT AND I'LL SHOW YA.
ZAK
OH!
OOPS. SORRY, HUNSACKER.
AHHH!
NOT
"PETER?"

The Following Monday.
MIDTOWN HIGH.
OHMIGOD! HE'S HERE!
ALPHA!
DUDE'S HOOKING ME UP WITH A FREE PHONE.
HEAR HE'S HANGING WITH TONY STARK!
HEY, ALPHA!
PARTY AT MY PLACE FRIDAY! YOU GOTTA COME!
HE LOOKED RIGHT AT ME!
DIDN'T SEE YOU THERE.

...HERE COMES
ALPHA!"
GET READY FOR THE NEXT SUPER-POWERED PRODUCT FROM HORIZON!
THE ALL-NEW AMAZING aPHONE!
IT'S GRADE A!
ALPHA-FAST!
AND ALPHA-TOUGH!
PYOO! PYOO! PYOO!
ZZAKK
AND IT BLOWS ALL OTHER SMART PHONES AWAY!
SO IF YOU WANT SUPER-CLEAR CALLS AT A SUPER-PRICE...
...TAKE IT FROM A HERO WHO ALWAYS ANSWERS THE CALL...
...THE ONE AND ONLY ALPHA!
IT'S GOING TO BE THE BEST-SELLING ITEM THIS QUARTER! WE SHOULD BE GETTING A CUT OF THAT!
I'M ON IT, OKAY?
LOOK WHO SUDDENLY HAS AN INTEREST IN OUR SON'S LIFE!
WHAT? I'VE ALWAYS

HERE'S WHAT WE'RE PREPARED TO OFFER: ALL MEDICAL EXPENSES...
REGULAR MONITORING OF HIS SUPERHUMAN PHYSIOGNOMY BY THE BEST SCIENTIFIC MINDS IN THE WORLD.
AND A LUCRATIVE CONTRACT--
A CONTRACT? WHAT ARE WE TALKING ABOUT HERE?
WE'D LIKE TO GROOM ANDREW TO BE OUR NEW CORPORATE SPOKESMAN. A SPOKES-SUPER HERO, IF YOU WILL.
ALPHA, THE NEW FACE OF HORIZON LABS.
A REAL SUPER HERO? LIKE AN AVENGER OR SOMETHING?
ANDY, FIRST WE--
YES! APPROVED!
HOW MUCH ARE WE TALKING?
OVER TIME, MORE THAN YOU'D MAKE IN ANY SETTLEMENT.
WE SHOULD TAKE THIS.
TOO COOL!
TOO COOL!
TOO COOL!
THIS WAS REED RICHARDS' IDEA?
ABSOLUTELY. AND YOU'LL BE PLAYING AN IMPORTANT PART IN IT, MR. PARKER, OVERSEEING THE ENTIRE ALPHA PROJECT...
"DESIGNING HIS GEAR, AND WORKING SIDE-BY-SIDE WITH HIM. JUST LIKE YOU DO FOR SPIDER-MAN."
ONE SCIENTIFIC MISHAP, AND HOURS LATER I'M SEWING A COSTUME.
DÉJÀ DIDDLY VU.
OKAY WORLD, BETTER HANG ON TO YOUR HAT...

THAT WHENEVER THE HULK, SENTRY OR THE PHOENIX ATTACKS...
...WE CALL IT AN OMEGA-LEVEL THREAT...
...ANDY MAGUIRE IS THE FIRST ALPHA-LEVEL THREAT. IT'S ONLY A MATTER OF TIME.
WHY DID I HAVE TO GO AND DO THIS?
DISCOVER "PARKER PARTICLES"? YOU DIDN'T. I DID. YEARS AGO.
WHAT?!
BUT I KNEW THAT THERE ARE SOME GENIES YOU DON'T LET OUT OF THE BOTTLE.
YOU ARE LUCKY THOUGH, PETER. IT'S A FLUKE THE BOY SURVIVED.
BUT NOW HE'S YOUR RESPONSIBILITY. YOU'LL HAVE TO KEEP AN EYE ON HIM. AND TRAIN HIM.
WAIT, BUT GIANT-MAN HAS A WHOLE SUPER HERO ACADEMY--
MAYBE DOWN THE ROAD. BUT FOR NOW, ANDY'S THE ALPHA. HE'S GOING TO NEED ONE-ON-ONE. YOU OPENED THAT DOOR. AND AS FOR HANK...
KID! PUT ME DOWN! NOW!
WAIT! I BET I CAN DO THIS WITH ONE HAND.
...SOMETHING TELLS ME, THE BOY'S A LITTLE MORE THAN HANK CAN HANDLE.
AGREED. SO HOW DO WE SWING THIS?
LET ME TALK TO MAX. I HAVE AN IDEA.

PROJECTION. CHECK.
PYOO! PYOO! PYOO!
ZZZRAK
1 TON
STRENGTH AUGMENTATION.
HEY, ARE THE OLYMPICS STILL GOING ON?
NO!
SUPER-SPEED.
AWESOME! SO? WHATCHA GOT NEXT?
FORCE FIELD.
WE DO THIS ALL THE TIME TO STUDENTS AT MY SCHOOL.
AHH! IS THIS SAFE?
YEAH? NO OFFENSE, MR. BEAST, BUT YOUR SCHOOL'S MESSED UP!
WHAT? LIKE THIS AIN'T NOUGH? NO FFENSE, MR. ODELL, BUT THIS--
--WILL NEVER GET OLD!
WHAT'S THE VERDICT? IS HE OKAY?
YES. HE HAS THE POWER UNDER CONTROL. THOUGH THERE IS A LIMITATION...
...IT APPEARS HE CAN ONLY MANIFEST ONE ABILITY AT A TIME.
I DON'T THINK "LIMITATION" IS THE RIGHT WORD HERE. PETER? A MOMENT.
SOMETHING YOU SHOULD KNOW. ANDY'S POWER IS TIED TO THE VERY UNIVERSE ITSELF. IT WILL CONTINUE TO GROW. WITHOUT LIMIT.
WHAT ARE YOU SAYING?

THIS ALL SORTED OUT."
MR. FANTASTIC
PROF. REED RICHARDS
LEVELS INCREASING AT A CONSTANT RATE.
THE BEAST
DR. HANK McCOY
CHECK.
IRON MAN
TONY STARK
GIANT-MAN
DR. HENRY PYM
"PARKER PARTICLES"?
GIVE IT A REST, PYM.
YOU OKAY IN THERE, ANDY?
YOU BET!
WHEN THIS IS DONE, CAN I GET EVERYBODY'S AUTOGRAPH?
SURE THING, KID.
THIS "ENERGY SOURCE," IT'S PERMEATED EVERY CELL OF HIS BODY...
...CHARGING AND RECHARGING THEM, BUT ACCORDING TO INITIAL SCANS...
...HE SHOULD BE ABLE TO RELEASE IT IN A NUMBER OF STANDARD SUPERHUMAN WAYS.

THE *BEST!*
DAY!
EVER!

ours later.

ORIZON LABS,
ONFERENCE ROOM #1.

OUR SON WAS THE VICTIM OF A MAJOR *INDUSTRIAL ACCIDENT!*

WHAT WAS HE EVEN *DOING* HERE?!

HORIZON IS COMPLETELY AT FAULT!

THIS DOESN'T *LOOK* LIKE YOUR SIGNATURE, RAY.

MS. CONWAY!

TORS HAVE CKED THE OY OUT.

APPEARS BE FINE. ERHUMAN, N FACT.

WHAT ABOUT *LONG-TERM* EFFECTS, MR. BAEZ?

WHO KNOWS WHAT YOUR COMPANY'S DONE TO ANDREW?!

WHAT IF SHE'S RIGHT?
AND WHAT ABOUT HORIZON?
I MIGHT'VE RUINED THINGS FOR EVERYBODY.

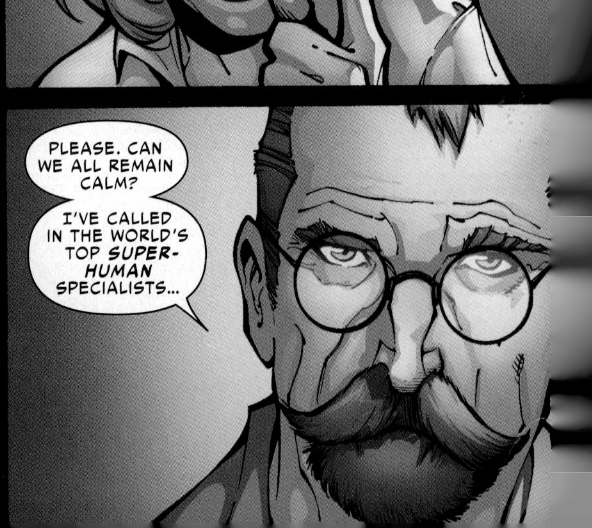

PLEASE. CAN WE ALL REMAIN CALM?
I'VE CALLED IN THE WORLD'S TOP SUPER-HUMAN SPECIALISTS...

WAIT! HE'S MOVING. IS HE ALL RIGHT?
FEEL... FUNNY...
RANDY? YOU OKAY?
RMMB
ANDY... NAME'S ANDY...
OH MY. I'M SORRY. ARE YOU--?
WATCH OUT!
I GOT IT!
ZZRAK
DID HE JUST--?
LIKE SOME KINDA SUPER HERO.

--CLEAR!
WHAT WAS I THINKING?!
AHHH!
STAY DOWN!
WHO'S LEFT?
IS THERE ANYONE I MISSED?!
OH, I KNOW EXACTLY WHAT I WAS THINKING!
I WAS SHOWING OFF TO ALL THE YOUNG FLASH THOMPSONS AND LIZ ALLANS OF THE WORLD!
LETTING 'EM SEE WHAT A BIG SHOT I'VE BECOME.
BECAUSE OF THAT...
CHRISSY!
...I PUT ALL OF THEM AT RISK!
LOOK OUT!
DEAR GOD, IF ANYTHING HAPPENS, THIS'LL ALL BE MY--
YEARGH---

IF WE HARNESS THIS ENERGY RIGHT, NOT TO TOOT MY OWN HORN, BUT THIS COULD...
...CHANGE THE WORLD.
SAFETIES DISENGAGED
WAIT. THAT'S...
...NOT GOOD.
SPIDER-SENSE TINGLING!
ZRAK-ZAK-ZAK-AK
SHUTTING EVERYTHING DOWN!
NO! THERE' TOO MUCH C A RESIDUAL CHARGE!
EVERYONE!
FIND COVER!
NOW!
SECRET IDENT BE DAMNED!
HAVE TO DO WHATEVER I CAN GET THESE KIDS

THE DAY I
ALLY SHOW
HEM ALL...
HI! WELCOME TO HORIZON LABS. I'M PETER PARKER, ONE-TIME MIDTOWN HIGH STUDENT, JUST LIKE YOU.
AND I WANTED YOU TO SEE THIS TODAY--TO KNOW THAT FROM WHERE YOU ARE RIGHT NOW--
--LITERALLY EVERYTHING IN THE UNIVERSE IS POSSIBLE!
THIS IS MY GREATEST DISCOVERY. REED RICHARDS FOUND UNSTABLE MOLECULES. HANK PYM, THE PYM PARTICLE. TONY STARK, ARC REACTOR TECHNOLOGY...
...BUT THIS IS ALL MINE. YOU ARE ABOUT TO SEE PARKER PARTICLES.
A HYPER-KINETIC FORM OF ENERGY TIED INTO THE FORCES OF UNIVERSAL EXPANSION ITSELF.
CLEAN, AFFORDABLE, NEAR-LIMITLESS POWER.
AND WE'RE SHOWING IT OFF TO HIGH SCHOOL STUDENTS.
YES, MR. STONE. AND TOP SCIENTISTS. THE MEDIA. POLICY MAKERS.
AFTER OUR...FIASCO WITH DR. MORBIUS AND THE LIZARD, A LITTLE GOOD PUBLICITY COULDN'T HURT.
MR. MODELL, ABOUT THAT...
NOW THAT DR. MORBIUS IS GONE...
...THERE'S AN OPENING IN YOUR PRIVATE THINK TANK, ISN'T THERE?
YES. AND I'M REVIEWING A NUMBER OF CANDIDATES.
YOU'RE A GOOD MAN, TIBERIUS. BUT NOW MIGHT NOT BE THE BEST TIME.
PERHAPS WHEN THE NEXT SPOT OPENS.
SAFETIES DISENGAGED
CLIK
I HEAR YOU, MAX. LOUD AND CLEAR.

E ATTENDING A DEMONSTRATION IN RADIOLOGY, SCHOOL SCIENCE STUDENT PETER PARKER WAS ENTALLY BITTEN BY A RADIOACTIVE SPIDER!

PETER SOON DISCOVERED THAT HE HAD GAINED THE SPIDER'S PROPORTIONATE STRENGTH, AGILITY, AND ABILITY TO STICK TO WALLS. HE HAD, IN EFFECT BECOME A HUMAN SPIDER!
PETER THOUGHT HE COULD USE THESE POWERS TO BECOME RICH AND FAMOUS.

HEN HE SELFISHLY ED TO HELP STOP LAR...

...WHO LATER SHOT AND KILLED PETER'S UNCLE BEN IN AN ATTEMPTED ROBBERY...
...PETER PARKER LEARNED THAT WITH GREAT POWER MUST ALSO COME GREAT RESPONSIBILITY. AND FROM THAT DAY FORTH, HE HAS USED HIS POWERS TO HELP PEOPLE AS...

AMAZING
PIDER-MAN
AGE BY VAN LENTE, ROMITA JR, JANSON AND WHITE

alpha
PART I:
POINT OF
ORIGIN
GREAT POWER. GREAT RESPONSIBILITY. A TEEN OUTCAST. ALL THE ELEMENTS OF A MODERN DAY MYTH IN THE MAKING, RIGHT?
WELL, THINK AGAIN, TRUE BELIEVER. BECAUSE THIS IS AN ALL-NEW TALE FOR THE TELLING.
AND WHILE THIS MAY BE MIDTOWN HIGH, THIS YOUNG MAN IS NO PETER PARKER.
HIS NAME'S ANDY MAGUIRE. AND, FOR THE MOMENT, THIS IS HIS STORY.

...AFTER WE KILL THE GEEKS!
NEXT: GET THAT NERD!

AMAZING SPIDER-MAN #697
COVER BY STEVE MCNIVEN & SIMON WEST

OFF AS THE HOBGOBLIN? YOU CAN'T EVEN KILL A COUPLE OF GEEKS!
GEEKS WHO BUILD WEAPONS FOR SPIDER-MAN! AND I DON'T SEE YOU DOING ANY BETTER, OLD MAN!
PETER! THE GOBLIN KEY IS PINGING--GETTING LOUDER! I THINK IT'S LEADING US TO NORMAN OSBORN'S SECRET CACHE!
PING PING
THEN FOLLOW IT, MAX! I'M BETTING OSBORN'S GOT THOSE FILES IN SOME KIND OF PANIC ROOM. IF WE CAN GET IN, WE'LL BE SAFE!
DANGER ZONE
PART THREE: WAR OF THE GOBLINS
LOTT & GAGE WRITERS
CAMUNCOLI PENCILS
GREEN & DELL INKS
FABELA COLORS
ELIOPOULOS LETTERER
McNIVEN & WEST COVER
AND I'M NOT SURE HOW MUCH LONGER I CAN PROTECT US. KINGPIN AND TIBERIUS STONE SET UP SPIDER-JAMMERS ALL OVER THE CITY. I WRECKED THE MAIN ONE BACK THERE...
...BUT THE FURTHER AWAY WE GET, THE MORE THE OTHERS RAMP MY SPIDER-SENSE INTO

WATCH AND LEARN, PUNK.
WHHTT
THWIP
NO! I MISSED-- AND IT'S HEADING STRAIGHT FOR--
MAX!
HM?
TOINK
COFFEE BAGEL DONUT 1.25
OH.
DIDN'T I MENTION MY FORCE FIELD?
IT'S A PROTOTYPE PROTECTION SYSTEM FOR FIRST RESPONDERS. I WASN'T GOING INTO THE LION'S DEN DEFENSELESS.
ONLY PROBLEM IS-- IT'S RUNNING ON MY CELL PHONE BATTERY, AND IT'LL BURN OUT SOON. BUT FOR NOW, GET IN FRONT OF ME. IT'LL PROTECT US BOTH.
YOU'RE DEFINITELY A GENIUS, MAX. WE'VE GOT A CHANCE AS LONG AS IT--AND THE WEB-SHOOTERS YOU BROUGHT ME--HOLD OUT...

...AND AS LONG AS NEW COKE HOBGOBLIN AND CLASSIC HOBGOBLIN ARE FIGHTING EACH OTHER AS MUCH AS US!
I'M OUT OF BOMBS! GIMME YOUR BAG, GRAMPA--
HEY!
HANDS OFF, WANNABE!
VZZATT
GAH! THAT'S IT. I DON'T CARE WHAT THE KINGPIN SAYS...
...YOU'RE A DEAD MAN!
IF THAT'S HOW YOU WANNA PLAY IT. BUT REMEMBER...
"...I'VE GOT A BAT-DRONE LOADED WITH C4 TAILING YOUR SWEETIE-PIE, NORAH.
"YOU MESS WITH THE ALPHA DOG AND IT'LL BE RAINING PIECES OF HER ALL OVER THE WEST SIDE HIGHWAY."

DEET DEET DEET
PETER! THE GOBLIN KEY'S GOING CRAZY!
WE'RE SPITTING DISTANCE FROM THE OSCORP BUILDNG. NORMAN WOULD WANT HIS SECRET STASH CLOSE BY.
I THINK I CAN BE MORE SPECIFIC.
THERE!
MOVE!
DAMN IT!
TOOK YOUR EYE OFF THE BALL. ROOKIE MISTAKE.
WILL. YOU. SHUT. UP!
RELAX. WE'LL GET IN. AND IF OSBORN'S VAULT IS ANYTHING LIKE THE ONE I BROKE INTO BACK IN THE DAY...
...THERE'S A PRETTY GOOD CHANCE THOSE TWO IDIOTS WILL BE DEAD WHEN WE DO.

OH...MY.
THIS MAKES YOUR CACHE OF SPIDER-MAN'S EQUIPMENT LOOK LIKE A STREET VENDOR'S TABLE.
WELL... I MEAN, NORMAN'S RICH.
IF YOU PAID ME MORE, I COULD HAVE SOMETHING LIKE THIS.
HELLO. WELCOME TO THE GOBLIN'S WORKSHOP. I'M NORMAN OSBORN.
IF YOU'RE SEEING THIS, YOU'RE NOT ME. WHICH IS UNFORTUNATE FOR YOU ON SO MANY LEVELS.
EASY. IT'S A HOLOGRAM.
NOT THE LEAST OF WHICH IS, IF YOU FAIL TO ENTER THE AUTHORIZATION CODE IN SIXTY SECONDS, THIS ENTIRE FACILITY, WHICH YOU MAY BE ASSURED IS ON TOTAL LOCKDOWN...
...WILL SELF-DESTRUCT. WITH YOU IN IT.

Seattle, Washington.

DEETLE DEET

JUST ANSWERING THIS CALL MEANS I HAVE TO MOVE AGAIN.
I'M SORRY, HARRY. BUT THIS IS REALLY AN EMERGENCY.
DO YOU KNOW THE SECURITY CODE FOR SOMETHING CALLED THE GOBLIN'S WORKSHOP? HATE TO RUSH YOU, BUT I'M KINDA ON THE CLOCK HERE.

UNLESS DAD CHANGED IT SINCE MY GOBLIN DAYS, IT'S "STROMM."
THE FIRST BUSINESS PARTNER HE SCREWED OVER. HE'S SENTIMENTAL LIKE THAT.

DID IT WORK, PETE? PETE...?
HNH.
SIGNAL LOST

HEY, STANLEY, I EVER TELL YOU ABOUT MY FRIEND PETER?
NICE GUY, BUT HE CAN NEVER SEEM TO GET THE DRAMA OUT OF HIS LIFE. UNLIKE US, RIGHT, BUDDY?
C'MON, LET'S GO FEED THE BIRDS.

VERY GOOD. CLEARLY I WANT YOU TO HAVE WHAT'S IN HERE. AND CLEARLY YOU POSSESS THE NECESSARY QUALITIES TO PUT IT TO GOOD USE.
HAVE FUN.
WHAT NOW? MY CELL PHONE'S ALMOST OUT OF POWER. SHOULD WE CALL THE POLICE? THE FANTASTIC FOUR? DOES SPIDER-MAN HAVE A CELL?
I HATE TO SAY IT, MAX...
"...BUT I'M NOT SURE ANYONE CAN GET HERE IN TIME."
BKRAMMMM
ALMOST THROUGH, JUNIOR.
YEAH, BUT IT'S TAKING TOO LONG.
I'VE GOT AN IDEA.
HEY, PARKER! YOU BETTER OPEN UP! WE'VE GOT A BAT-DRONE FULL OF EXPLOSIVES AIMED AT YOUR FRIEND, NORAH WINTERS!
GIVE US WHAT'S IN THAT VAULT! OR SHE'S GONNA BE ABSTRACT ART ALONG THE WEST SIDE HIGHWAY!
WHAT'S IT GONNA BE, PARKER? TICK, TICK TICK...
YOU MEAN IT, DON'T YOU?
NOT BAD, KID. NOW YOU'RE GETTING YOUR PRIORITIES IN ORDER.
YOU MIGHT JUST HAVE A FUTURE AT THIS.

HOW DO WE KNOW YOU WON'T KILL US AND THEN KILL HER ANYWAY?
USE YOUR HEAD, PARKER! ALL WE WANT IS OSBORN'S STASH! YOU THREE CAN GO FLY A KITE FOR ALL WE CARE!
I REALIZE YOU'RE JUST BUYING TIME, BUT MAYBE WE SHOULD CONSIDER NEGOTIATING.

DON'T KID YOURSELF, MAX. THEY'D MURDER US ALL WITHOUT THINKING TWICE.
BUT THIS EQUIPMENT...WE'VE HAD SO LITTLE TIME, AND IT'S SO COMPLEX--
I HELPED SPIDER-MAN BUILD A VERSION OF THIS. THE "SPIDER-GLIDER." I'M USED TO IT.

ANYWAY, IT'S NOT ROCKET SCIENCE. I'LL PUT THIS ON, PRETEND TO BE SPIDER-MAN, DISTRACT THEM, YOU GET OUT. AND BRING HELP FOR ME...AND NORAH!
"PRETEND" TO BE SPIDER-MAN. BECAUSE THAT'S SO SIMPLE.
I'VE DONE IT BEFORE...

"...AS FAR BACK AS HIGH SCHOOL.*"
*THAT'S WHAT PETE TOLD EVERYONE WHEN DOC OCK UNMASKED HIM IN ASM #12! -FLASHWACK WACKER.

I'M NOT SAYING IT WORKED OUT GREAT...
...BUT ALL I HAVE TO DO THIS TIME IS RUN FOR MY LIFE. WHICH I THINK I CAN MANAGE...
...UNLESS SOMETHING ELSE GOES WRONG.

MY PATIENCE IS RAPIDLY RUNNING OUT, STONE. I WANT THE HOBGOBLIN COMPLETELY FOCUSED ON RETRIEVING THE GOBLIN KEY.
YOUR DEVICE WAS MEANT TO PREVENT SPIDER-MAN'S INTERFERENCE. IF YOU CAN'T DELIVER ON THAT PROMISE--
Shadowland.
THE KINGPIN'S STRONGHOLD.
WAIT! IT'S WORKING!
DON'T WORRY, MR. FISK. NOW THAT THE MASTER SPIDER-JAMMER'S FUNCTIONING AGAIN, HIS SPIDER-SENSE IS BACK ON OVERDRIVE. WHEREVER SPIDER-MAN IS....
"...HE'S IN AGONY!"
NNAAHH!
PETER!
MIGRAINE... ROM THE STRESS.
I'M AFRAID YOU'LL HAVE TO FIGHT THROUGH IT. THE HOBGOBLINS HAVE BEGUN TRYING TO BREAK IN AGAIN. FROM THE SOUNDS, WE DON'T HAVE LONG.
I'M...F-FINE. LOOK, OSBORN ALWAYS HAS A BACKUP PLAN. CHECK THE COMPUTER...SEE IF YOU CAN FIND SCHEMATICS FOR THIS PLACE. THERE MIGHT BE ANOTHER EXIT...
I'LL DO MY BEST. THE GOOD NEWS IS, HE HASN'T BOTHERED WITH MUCH ENCRYPTION... APPARENTLY THE SELF-DESTRUCT SYSTEM WAS HIS FIREWALL.
THANK GOD...COULDN'T HIDE THE PAIN ANY LONGER. I THOUGHT THIS WAS BAD BEFORE, BUT WITH TWO HOBGOBLINS COMING TO KILL ME, IT'S EXCRUCIATING.
MY SPIDER-SENSE HAS SAVED MY LIFE A MILLION TIMES. BUT NOW IT'S GOING TO BE THE DEATH OF BOTH OF US.

AN ESCAPE HATCH BEHIND THE TARGET DUMMIES. THE UNLOCK MECHANISM'S CODED...
S-SEE IF YOU CAN CRACK IT.
"FIGHT THROUGH IT," MAX SAID. HOW DO YOU FIGHT THROUGH YOUR BRAIN FEELING LIKE IT'S EXPLODING OUT OF YOUR SKULL?
NEVER THOUGHT I'D MISS THE DAYS WHEN I LOST MY SPIDER-SENSE. I MADE OUT FINE, AFTER SHANG-CHI TAUGHT ME MARTIAL ARTS--
WAIT. THAT TRAINING--IT WAS ALL ABOUT MASTERING MY BODY. UNDERSTANDING IT, AND EXCEEDING ITS LIMITATIONS.
THIS IS NO DIFFERENT THAN THE PAIN OF A BROKEN BONE. GOT TO FOCUS...
...BLOCK IT OUT. PUT UP A WALL AROUND MY SPIDER-SENSE... SEAL IT OFF...
...JUST WISH IT DIDN'T HURT SO MUCH...
YES! THE HATCH IS OPEN.
I'VE REACTIVATED THE SELF-DESTRUCT SEQUENCE ON A TE MINUTE TIMER-- REGARDLESS OF WHAT HAPPENS, NO ONE WILL GET WHAT'S IN HERE.
AND WITH THE SCHEMATICS I'VE FOUND FOR THE BAT DRONE TECH, I THIN I CAN TRACK NORAH THROUGH THE DRONE THAT'S FOLLOWING HER.
EVERYTHING'S SET, PETER. ARE YOU READY?
LET'S DO THIS.

SHRRAKK
ONE MORE WHACK OUGHTA DO IT.
HEY, GUYS, I LOVE YOUR OUTFITS.
GLIDERS AND BOMBS ARE THE HOT TREND RIGHT NOW.
SPIDER-MAN? BEEN A WHILE, HASN'T IT, BUG?
NO WAY! HOW ARE YOU EVEN STANDING? STONE SAID YOUR BRAINS'D BE BOILING OUTTA YOUR EARS BY NOW!
SORRY, ZIPPY. DIDN'T GET THAT MEMO.
NOW WHICH ONE ARE YOU SUPPOSED TO BE? LEEDS? MACENDALE? OR--
HEY! I KNOW THAT CHEEKBONE ANYWHERE. RODDY! HOW'S TRICKS?
SO FAR, SO GOOD...NO SPIDER-SENSE WARNING ME OF ATTACKS, BUT IT'S NOT PLAYING IRON MAIDEN IN MY HEAD EITHER.
NOW ALL I HAVE TO DO IS SURVIVE AGAINST TWO HOBGOBLINS...

HEY! YOU ALMOST HIT ME!
WOULD ONE DEADLY THREAT AT A TIME BE TOO MUCH TO ASK?
STILL WAITING TO HEAR THE DOWNSIDE.
I HAVE SPIDER-MAN FIGHTING THE HOBGOBLIN NEAR THE OSCORP BUILDING! WAIT, MAKE THAT TWO HOBGOBLINS!
--ALL UNITS IN THE VICINITY, RESPOND. PERPETRATORS IDENTIFIED AS THE HOBGOBLIN--
POLICE
--AND SPIDER-MAN.
POLICE

I AM SO GONNA KILL YOU BOTH FOR THIS!
KILLING--GOOD IDEA. IT'S TIME SPIDER-MAN GOT A REMINDER WHAT HAPPENS WHEN HE CROSSES THE REAL HOBGOBLIN.
PEOPLE DIE.
STARTING WITH NORAH WINTERS.
NO!
HUH. I THOUGHT HIM BLOWING NORAH TO BITS WOULD BOTHER ME. BUT ALL I CAN THINK IS...
HA! NOW THE SHOE'S ON THE OTHER FOOT!
HOW DO YOU LIKE BEING COLLATERAL DAMAGE, OLD MAN?
I DON'T NEED SPIDER-SENSE TO TELL ME I'M A SITTING DUCK LIKE THIS. BUT I CAN'T LET GO.
GOTTA BUY MAX AS MUCH TIME AS I CAN...

...AND PRAY NORAH'S CLOSE BY!
BEDEEP
COBRETT

÷HUFF÷ ÷HUFF÷ THERE...
OH, NO.
COBRETT

AAAA!
NEW YORK LET'S CLEAN UP

WHOOOOM

WHAT THE HECK--? YOU'RE MAX MODELL!
UH, YES. AND YOU'VE JUST HELPED ME BETA-TEST MY FORCE FIELD APP.

TOO LATE! SHE'S DEAD-- DDH!
YOU'D BETTER HOPE FOR YOUR SAKE YOU'RE WRONG.
HOW ABOUT THIS?
YOU'RE BOTH DEAD! AND OSBORN'S FILES ARE ALL MINE!
HAHAHA HAHA--
BRAKKA
BOOOOM

NNH...
PETER? I HAVE NORAH! SHE'S SAFE!
M-MAX? YOU DON'T KNOW HOW GOOD THAT IS TO HEAR.

THEY BLEW IT UP. I DON'T FREAKIN' BELIEVE IT.
THAT'S IT. I SAY THE TRUCE IS BACK ON. THIS PUNK NEEDS TO DIE.
SOUNDS GOOD TO ME.

WELL, NOT ME.
THE GIRL'S SAFE, MY TECH GUYS ARE SAFE, AND OSBORN'S STUFF IS SO MUCH ASH. I'M OUTTA HERE. YOU WANNA KEEP BEATING ON EACH OTHER, MAKE MY DAY.

WHAT? YOU BELIEVE THIS COWARD? LET'S GET HIM.
Y'KNOW WHAT?

NAH.
SHHAKKK

D-DOUBLE-
CROSSING--

WELL, *THAT* DIDN'T TAKE LONG.

NEITHER ONE'S COMING UP...WHICH PROBABLY MEANS THEY BOTH SWAM OFF TO LICK THEIR WOUNDS. NOT BAD ADVICE.
I SHOULD LOOK FOR 'EM, BUT I CAN BARELY STAND. THINK I'LL CALL IT A DAY AND COUNT MYSELF LUCKY NOBODY GOT SERIOUSLY HURT...

YOU LOOK KINDA *GREEN,* KID. OH, THAT'S RIGHT--I DIDN'T PUT AN OXYGEN SUPPLY IN THAT REDESIGNED SUIT. GUESS MY OLD STUFF *WAS* BETTER.
IF YOU'RE...GONNA KILL ME...JUST SHUT UP AND DO IT.

I *WAS* GOING TO. BUT YOU SHOWED ME *POTENTIAL* TODAY, SO I'LL GIVE YOU A CHANCE TO LIVE. AND EVEN KEEP BEING THE HOBGOBLIN.
W-WHAT'S THE CATCH? WHAT'S IN IT FOR YOU?
A CUT.
THE UNKINDEST CUT OF ALL...

Shadowland.
ALL CONTENTS OF OSBORN'S VAULT WERE DESTROYED, MASTER. BURNED BEYOND RETRIEVAL.
DESTROYED...

...BECAUSE OF SPIDER-MAN!
STONE SWORE TO ME HIS WORTHLES DEVICE WOULD CRIPPLE SPIDER-MAN WHERE IS THAT CHARLATAN? BRING HIM TO ME IMMEDIATELY!
HE CLAIMED HE NEEDED TO RETURN TO HIS LABORATORY FOR PARTS. WE HAVE MEN POSTED NEAR HIS HOME, HIS WORKPLACE AND ALL LOCATIONS HE FREQUENTS.
BRASH

"YOU HAVE MY SOLEMN VOW, MASTER...
BEDOOP

"...TIBERIUS STONE HAS NOWHERE TO RUN."
Stone: You're fired. Max.

THERE. I THINK THAT TEXT WAS WORTH THE LAST OF MY BATTERY POWER.
HEY, ARE YOU TWO OKAY?

WE'RE FINE, SPIDER-MAN. AM I CORRECT IN CALLING YOU THAT?
YEAH, IT'S ME. PARKER FILLED ME IN, ASKED ME TO CHECK ON YOU. HE'S SAFE TOO.
WELL, GOOD. I'M GLAD YOU'RE *BOTH* OUT OF DANGER.
UH, THANKS.
DOES MAX *KNOW?* HE IS A GENIUS...AH, THE HECK WITH IT. I'VE GOT MORE IMMEDIATE PROBLEMS...

SPIDER-MAN! CAN I GET AN INTERVIEW?
CALL THE AVENGERS' PRESS AGENT.
...LIKE GOING AROUND TOWN AND TAKING OUT THOSE SPIDER-JAMMERS.
'CAUSE I'D REALLY LIKE TO BE ABLE TO TRUST MY SPIDER-SENSE AGAIN.

FUNNY. KEEP FEELING I GOT OFF EASY THIS TIME.
MADAME WEB MADE IT SOUND LIKE THE WORLD WAS ABOUT TO END. GUESS EVEN SHE HAS OFF DAYS.

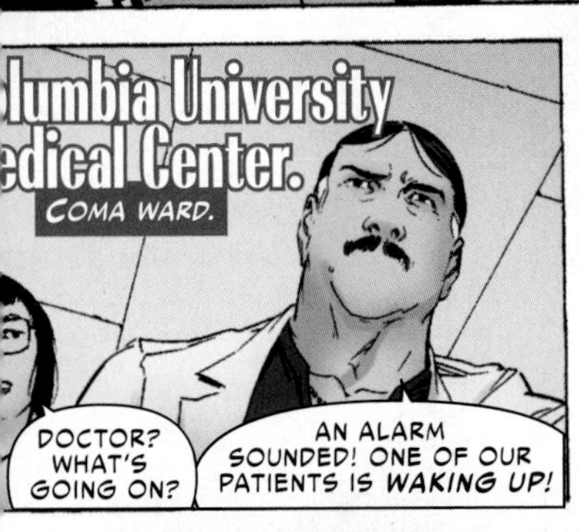

lumbia University
edical Center.
COMA WARD.
DOCTOR? WHAT'S GOING ON?
AN ALARM SOUNDED! ONE OF OUR PATIENTS IS *WAKING UP!*

WHO IS IT?

AND *WHERE DID HE GO?*
OSBORN,
NORMAN VIRGIL

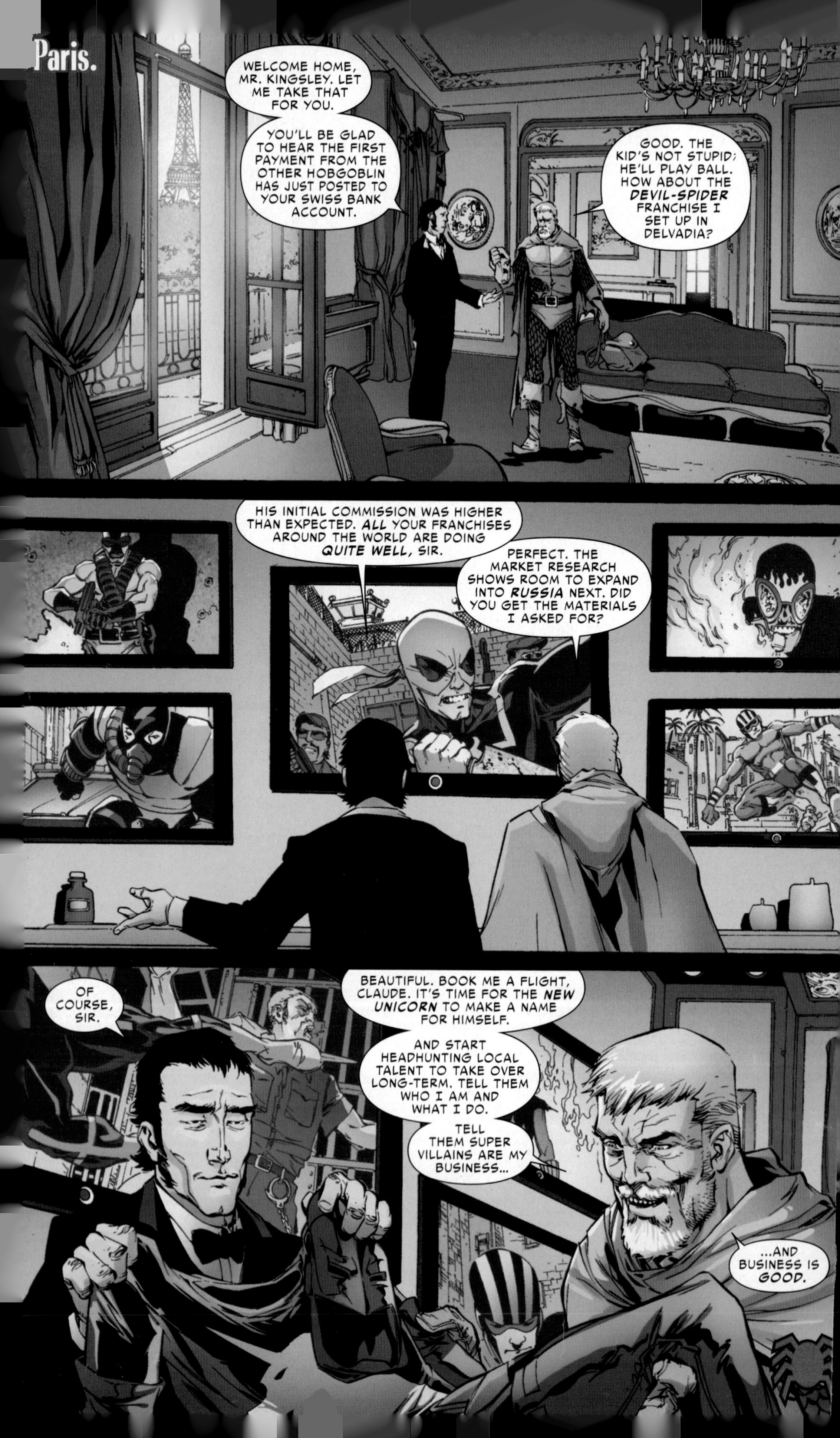
Paris.
WELCOME HOME, MR. KINGSLEY. LET ME TAKE THAT FOR YOU.
YOU'LL BE GLAD TO HEAR THE FIRST PAYMENT FROM THE OTHER HOBGOBLIN HAS JUST POSTED TO YOUR SWISS BANK ACCOUNT.
GOOD. THE KID'S NOT STUPID; HE'LL PLAY BALL. HOW ABOUT THE DEVIL-SPIDER FRANCHISE I SET UP IN DELVADIA?
HIS INITIAL COMMISSION WAS HIGHER THAN EXPECTED. ALL YOUR FRANCHISES AROUND THE WORLD ARE DOING QUITE WELL, SIR.
PERFECT. THE MARKET RESEARCH SHOWS ROOM TO EXPAND INTO RUSSIA NEXT. DID YOU GET THE MATERIALS I ASKED FOR?
OF COURSE, SIR.
BEAUTIFUL. BOOK ME A FLIGHT, CLAUDE. IT'S TIME FOR THE NEW UNICORN TO MAKE A NAME FOR HIMSELF.
AND START HEADHUNTING LOCAL TALENT TO TAKE OVER LONG-TERM. TELL THEM WHO I AM AND WHAT I DO.
TELL THEM SUPER VILLAINS ARE MY BUSINESS...
...AND BUSINESS IS GOOD.

AMAZING SPIDER-MAN #692 50TH ANNIVERSARY VARIANTS
COVERS BY MARCOS MARTIN

AMAZING SPIDER-MAN #692 50TH ANNIVERSARY VARIANTS

COVERS BY MARCOS MARTIN

AMAZING SPIDER-MAN #692
50TH ANNIVERSARY VARIANT
COVER BY MARCOS MARTIN

MAZING SPIDER-MAN #692
N EXPO VARIANT
OVER BY J. SCOTT CAMPBELL
EDGAR DELGADO

Hero was unleashed in the pages of Amazing Fantasy #15.*

*Comic historians will point out that AF #15 was actually "cover-dated" August, so the issue actually went on sale in June most likely, but we've chosen August as the date that most long-time fans recognize as the Anniversary. Besides we had a big Lizard story to get to in June and who has time to be pedantic when the Lizard is chasing after you?!

Although this is the 692nd issue of "Amazing Spider-Man," when you count all the issues of Spidey's various ongoing series (and exclude one-shots, mini-series, stories outside regular Marvel continuity, and odd numbered issues like #0 issues and POINT ONEs), this is — at least by super-intern Devin Lewis' count — the 1,757th comic Marvel has published featuring the ongoing drama of Peter Parker. That's a lot of thwips!

With 1,757 swings at the plate, there've been plenty of great Spidey issues (and, sure, even some lousy ones), but what's been consistent in every issue is the level of talent, heart and dedication that the men and women on this book have brought with them. We started this whole shebang with Stan, Steve, Artie and Jazzy John, but it's continued thanks to many others.

Through the years, the character has been guided by some of the greatest talent in the history of the comic medium. For this Fiftieth Anniversary, I want to just take a moment to say a massive "Thank You" to the giants whose shoulders we stand on (well I do more of a half-sitting/half-kneeling thing) each and every issue.

Truth is, though, there are lots of comics who have had great creative teams guiding the destinies of our favorite heroes. What's made the difference in Spidey's case is, without a doubt, the fans.

From comics to television to novels to newspaper strips to toys to movies to Broadway, Spidey's fans are sensational, spectacular, and downright amazing group.

From kids to adults worldwide, no character in history has ever reached a wider, more diverse audience. You want to waste a day? Try to find someone anywhere who has never at least heard of Spider-Man. They're a rare breed.

So to commemorate the passion of Spidey readers around the world who have supported the wall-crawler for five decades, I've turned to two of the proudest and loudest Spidey fanatics around to share their love and passion. Take it away, boys!

It was 1975. I was an 8-year-old kid riding his bike past the local 7-11, and I saw the sign that would change my life forever:

Spider-Man was coming to town.

That Saturday.

To sign comic books.

I loved Spidey. I raced home every day after school to watch reruns of the old '67 cartoons. And I knew what comics were, because my cousin collected them. But I never owned any. And now I HAD to have one, because I HAD to meet Spider-Man.

That night, the second my dad came home from his long commute, I was all over him. Pleading for a quarter so I could buy a Spider-Man comic. Dad asked if I was old enough to start doing chores around the house. Because if I was, I was old enough to get an allowance. A quarter a week. But he started me out with two — so I could have TWO comics for Spider-Man to sign.

I went back to the store extra early and pored over the spinner rack, looking for the two PERFECT Spider-Man comics. Those were MARVEL TALES #63 and MARVEL TEAM-UP #38. And then I camped out on the stoop, because I wanted to see Spider-Man swing in. I kid you not. I sat on the curb and kept looking up. Over time I got worried, because it was suburban California — there were NO tall buildings — so there was nothing for Spidey to stick a web to. I didn't know HOW he was going to get there.

And then it happened. The moment that sealed my fate and made me a Spidey fan for life. If you can imagine a couple of guys in the 70's who had access to a Spider-Man costume than this will make perfect sense. You could see the freeway and the off ramp from the 7-11, and there was a red pickup racing along, with Spider-Man — standing arms akimbo — in the bed of the truck. People who were stuck in traffic were cheering him on. It was surreal.

And the pickup drove down the exit, rolled into the parking lot, and — for my benefit alone — that crazy 70's guy in his Spider-Man suit, leapt out the back of the truck, landed in a spidery crouch, straightened himself up, and walked into that 7-11 like it was something he did ALL the time.

And I bought it. I believed. And he was great. He stayed in character, signed my books, and that was it for me. Spidey. Fan. For life.

It's 37 years later, and since then I've given tours of the Marvel Offices WITH Spidey (he says "Hi" by the way), written video game dialogue for Stan Lee and four of TV's animated Spider-Men, worked with the talented writers, artists, and editors of the Brand New Day team — and now the Big Time team. And look, we're here, on the 50th Anniversary issue… and it's all 'cause of you guys.

We get the honor and the privilege to be at this very special moment in Spidey history — and Humberto, Victor, Edgar, Chris, Ellie, and Steve, we all want you to know that we're very grateful for your patronage and your support. Thank you for letting us have these dream jobs.

See you in another 50! Thwip thwip!

Dan Slott
High above New York City

Dear ASM crew,

Wow! Fifty years of Spider-Man.

Though I've only been a serious reader of Spidey and comics in general for about a decade, without a doubt Spider-Man was the character that first drew me into the world of super heroes and brought me back after a brief h[illegible]atus from reading comics.

Like a lot of peop[illegible] age, my earliest memories of the web-slinge[illegible]obably came from the 90's cartoon. Maybe [illegible] things like the animation limits don't hold u[illegible] well, but for my money it's still a quintessent[illegible]ey adaptation with some of the best storytell[illegible]d characterizations. (Some perfect casting [illegible] like Ed Asner as J. Jonah Jameson who is [illegible] there with JK Simmons in my opinion.) P[illegible]s pretty much the gateway drug that introdu[illegible] the rest of the crazy world of Marvel like D[illegible]nge, Blade and Daredevil.

Over the year[illegible]t in Sp[illegible] started to wane until the[illegible] film in 2002[illegible] character ca[illegible]

in comics. I immediately got a Marvel subscr[illegible] to the Amazing Spider-Man title starting with #482 of the JMS/John Romita Jr. run and I ha[illegible] stopped reading and collecting since.

It's hard to pinpoint precisely what the dr[illegible] Spider-Man is out of all the supe heroes, but I [illegible] one of the reasons is, like Peter, we all at some [illegible] in our lives can't help but feel like a small b[illegible] a big world…especially those of us who have been a bit of a social misfit or outsider. Spide[illegible] come a long way since his early days as th[illegible] shy introverted kid in Amazing Fantasy #15 an[illegible] really come into his own as both a person [illegible] hero in the Marvel Universe.

The costume itself is also probably one [illegible] most iconic outfits in comics that allows prac[illegible] anyone to project themselves onto Spidey. As [illegible] as that original Stan Lee and Steve Ditko costu[illegible] readers can't help but enjoy when a new vari[illegible] look does pop for however length of time. I've [illegible] it no secret that I have a strong love of the Bom[illegible] Bag-Man costume, going so far as to dress [illegible] Bag-Man for Halloween. But whatever the loo[illegible] be, the hero inside will always remain true.

There's never been a better time to be a Spid[illegible] thanks hugely to what all of you guys at "S[illegible] Sentral" have accomplished in the last few [illegible] starting with Brand New Day and the work [illegible] various Web-heads to Dan Slott's solo run as [illegible] with "Big Time." It's all been a seamless and n[illegible] progression of everything that's come before.

Villains in particular, both new and old, [illegible] really stepped up and offer serious challeng[illegible] Spidey. The best villains are usually ones th[illegible] dark reflections of the hero and the "Great P[illegible] Responsibility" adage, which is why Phil Uric[illegible] quickly become my favorite person to take [illegible] Hobgoblin mantle. Same thing with Flash Thom[illegible] as the new Venom. It's funny because whe[illegible] Gargan/Scorpion got the symbiote I kept waiti[illegible] Eddie Brock to reclaim it, but now that Flash h[illegible] never want to see anyone BUT Flash be Venom[illegible]

You guys have not let up and that's why I [illegible] wait for what's coming up for the end of th[illegible] and beyond. As NYC citizens know well, 201[illegible] mayoral election year, so I'm eager to see ho[illegible] plays out within the pages for everyone's fa[illegible] skinflint JJJ. (I personally am holding out f[illegible] long awaited return of my favorite new S[illegible] villain: Paper Doll. What's taking so long, Dan!

So here's to the first Fifty years of Spidey a[illegible] with any luck — Fifty more! You guys at S[illegible] Sentral keep making 'em, and I'll keep reading[illegible]

Taimur Dar
a.k.a. Your Friendly Neighborhood Spidey616

And here's to fans like you, Taimur. Than[illegible] for your almost daily support of the book [illegible] appreciate all the terrific fans out there acros[illegible] world and across the internet.

Whether people love what we're doing or loa[illegible] with the white hot intensity of Brevoort's pas[illegible] filled beard, there's no doubting or denyin[illegible] intense passion Spidey brings out in othe[illegible] well-mannered people.

On behalf of Dan, Humberto, Victor, E[illegible] Chris, Manny, Stefano, Cammo, Klaus, Fra[illegible] Brennan, Ellie, Brevoort, Axel, Joe Q., and th[illegible] of the folks here in Spidey-land…I can ho[illegible] say we love ya all (but not in THAT way!)

And with that, I think we're done. It's ba[illegible] regular business next issue with part two [illegible] Alpha story and the continuing drama that is [illegible] to build all around Spidey culminating in the [illegible] to-be-disastrous ASM #700 in December.

Fifty years in … and we're goin' out with a b[illegible]

Viva[illegible]
Simperin'[illegible]